Quick

MW01253827

in Microsoft Office

Publisher

2003 Training Edition

Fast-track training® for busy people

Online Training Solutions, Inc.

PUBLISHED BY
Online Training Solutions, Inc.
PO Box 951
Bellevue, WA 98009-0951
E-mail: CustomerService@otsi.com
Web site: www.otsi.com

Publisher's Cataloging-in-Publication

Quick course in Microsoft Office Publisher 2003 :
  fast-track training for busy people / Online Training
Solutions, Inc. -- Training ed.
    p. cm. -- (Quick course)
    Includes index.
    LCCN 2005920473
    ISBN 978-1-58278-083-2

    1. Microsoft Publisher. 2. Desktop publishing.
I. Online Training Solutions (Firm) II. Title: Publisher
2003 III. Series: Quick course books.

  Z253.532.M53Q52 2005   686.2'2544536
                        QBI05-200067

Printed and bound in the United States of America

    3 4 5 6 7 8 9 P U B 3 2 1 0

Content overview

Introduction   viii

PART ONE: LEARNING THE BASICS

1 Creating Simple Publications   2

After a brief introduction, you create your first publication. You learn the
various parts of a publication, how to work with color schemes and text, and
how to save and print your work. Finally, you learn how to get help and quit
Publisher.

2 Developing More Complex Publications   40

You use a wizard to create a flyer and then rearrange its elements by working
with its frames. Then to see how to customize the flyer further, you take a look
at Publisher's formatting capabilities, including multiple columns, lists, and
styles.

3 Adding Visual Elements   76

This chapter shows you how to add graphics, borders, and special type effects
to your publications. Along the way you explore Publisher's Design Gallery and
use the drawing tools to create your own graphic objects.

PART TWO: BUILDING PROFICIENCY

4 Designing Longer Publications   110

While showing you how to create a newsletter, we discuss the design and editorial concepts you need to know to produce effective longer publications. Then
you develop and format tables from scratch and work with forms.

5 Creating Custom Templates   142

You design a template as you create a press release from scratch. Then you add
items to the background so that they can be repeated on every page, and
develop a custom color scheme. Finally, you create a publication based on your
template.

6 Using Advanced Printing and Publishing Techniques   166

You look at more ways to fine-tune your files, as well as handle final page
adjustments. Then you create materials for bulk mailings and prepare a publication for commercial printing. Finally, you use a wizard to create a Web page.

Index   194

Content details

Introduction   viii

PART ONE: LEARNING THE BASICS

1   Creating Simple Publications   2

Creating Your First Publication 4
   Choosing a Publication Type 4
   Filling In Your Personal Information 7
   Completing the Publication.................................. 9
Giving Publisher Instructions...................................... 10
   Using the Toolbars 10
   Repositioning a Toolbar 11
   Giving Menu Commands 13
Saving, Closing, and Opening Publications 14
   Saving a Publication 14
   Closing and Opening a Publication 15
Moving Around a Publication...................................... 16
   Moving to a Different Page 16
   Zooming In and Out 17
   Identifying Parts of a Publication 19
Working with Text 19
   Adding and Replacing Text................................ 19
   Editing Personal Information 21
   Deleting a Placeholder Text Box 21
   Moving and Copying Text 22
   Undoing and Redoing Commands 23
Using Task Panes to Make Design Changes 24
   Changing the Basic Design 25
   Changing the Color Scheme 26
Checking Spelling 27
   Checking the Spelling of One Word....................... 27
   Checking the Spelling of an Entire Publication 28
Printing Publications 30
Creating Other Simple Publications 31
   Creating a New Publication from an Existing One 32
   Designing a Business Card 33
   Making Adjustments to the Business Card 34
Getting Help 37
   Searching for Help... 38
Quitting Publisher... 39

2 Developing More Complex Publications

40

Creating Publications by Using Design Sets 42
   Creating a Flyer Based on a Master Sets Design 42
   Selecting Layout and Color Options 44
Reusing Information from Other Publications 45
   Adjusting the Personal Information Set 45
   Copying and Pasting Between Publications 46
Working with Text Boxes 47
   Sizing Text Boxes 47
   Adding and Deleting Text Boxes 49
   Moving Text Boxes 50
   Sizing Object Text Boxes 53
Formatting Words and Paragraphs 55
   Formatting Text 55
   Adding Borders 58
   Drawing Lines 59
   Adding Shading 60
   Changing Text Color 61
   Adding a Drop Cap 62
   Setting Up Multiple Columns 64
   Justifying Paragraphs 67
Working with Bulleted Lists 68
   Filling In a List 68
   Changing the Bullet Character in a Bulleted List 68
   Converting Existing Text to a Bulleted List 69
Formatting with Styles 70
   Creating a Style from Existing Text 71
   Creating a Style from Scratch 72
   Applying a Style 74

3 Adding Visual Elements

76

Creating a Brochure 78
   Starting a New Brochure 78
   Filling In the Brochure's Text Fields 79
Creating a Logo 80
   Inserting a Design Gallery Object 80
   Customizing a Design Gallery Object 82
Creating Fancy Text Effects with WordArt 83
   Creating a WordArt Object 83
   Customizing a WordArt Object 85
Working with Template Tables 87
   Modifying a Table Title 88
   Modifying Table Text 88
   Rebreaking Lines in a Table 89

Deleting a Table Row 90
Formatting a Table Column 90
Deleting a Table 91
Working with Graphics 93
Replacing a Placeholder Graphic 93
Searching for a Graphic 97
Sizing and Positioning a Graphic 99
Changing a Graphic's Color 100
Working with Shapes 102
Drawing a Shape 103
Working with a Group of Shapes 103
Changing a Shape's Color 105
Hiding and Displaying On-Screen Guides 107

PART TWO: BUILDING PROFICIENCY

4 Designing Longer Publications   110
Setting Up Newsletters 112
Creating a Newsletter by Using a Design Set 112
Adjusting the Page Layout 112
Making Design Decisions 114
Determining Who the Audience Is 115
Determining What's Most Important 116
Determining Which Graphics to Use 118
Working with Text in Longer Publications 119
Entering and Formatting Text 119
Editing Text in Microsoft Word 121
Flowing Text from Text Box to Text Box 122
Adding "Continued" Lines 123
Filling White Space 125
Adding Graphics to the Newsletter 125
Inserting an Attention Getter 126
Fine-Tuning the Newsletter's Content 127
Recycling a Logo 129
Creating Tables from Scratch 130
Inserting a New Table 130
Sizing Columns or Rows 132
Adding a Table Title 133
Coloring Cells 134
Adding Gridlines and a Border 135
Creating a Table of Contents 136
Working with Forms 137
Filling In Forms 137
Customizing a Form 138

5 Creating Custom Templates   **142**

Creating Publication Templates 144
 Creating a Publication to Use as a Template 144
 Saving a Publication as a Template 145
Adding Design Elements 146
 Inserting Graphics 146
 Inserting a Date Field 147
 Adding Text Boxes 148
 Inserting a Row of Dots 152
Working with the Master Page Layer 153
 Adding a Graphic to the Master Page 153
 Adding Headers and Footers 156
 Moving an Element to the Master Page 157
Creating Custom Color Schemes 158
 Changing the Colors in a Color Scheme 159
 Adding a Custom Color to the Color Scheme 160
 Applying Colors from the Color Scheme 162
Using Custom Templates 163
 Creating a Template-Based Publication 163
 Adding Text to a Template-Based Publication 164

6 Using Advanced Printing and Publishing Techniques   **166**

Making Final Adjustments 168
 Proofreading Your Work 168
 Adjusting the Page Setup 169
Printing Bulk Mailings 172
 Creating the Data Source 173
 Merging and Printing the Publication 175
Sending Publications to Printing Services 178
 Using the Pack and Go Wizard 180
 Creating a PostScript File 180
Creating Web Sites 181
 Using Publisher's Web Site Creation Tools 182
 Adding Text and Graphics to a Web Site 184
 Adding a Price List to a Web Site 186
 Adjusting Interactive Web Elements 187
 Adjusting the Background 189
 Previewing a Web Page 191

Index   **194**

Introduction

You probably have several business cards in your wallet, receive newsletters in the mail, and pick up the occasional flyer. The effectiveness of these pieces depends on their ability to catch your eye, hold your interest, and convey their message efficiently. Because you can use Microsoft Office Publisher 2003 to quickly and easily create publications that meet all these criteria, Publisher is rapidly becoming the preferred desktop-publishing software for small to medium-sized businesses and organizations, as well as individuals.

How do you generate publications that will look attractive and get the word out about your company or organization, about your product or service, or about an upcoming event? You could hire a professional designer to guide you and do most of the work. But suppose you don't have the budget. You need to be able to create functional, good-looking pieces yourself. That's where a sophisticated desktop-publishing package like Publisher comes in.

With Publisher, you can concentrate on the message of a publication and let the program handle many of the aesthetic details. Publisher can help with virtually every facet of creating a publication so that you can easily produce professional-quality documents. At the same time, Publisher allows you to tailor components to your own needs and tastes; you're never constrained by the program's idea of what a publication should look like.

Publisher's tools work much the same way as the tools in other programs in the Microsoft Office Suite, such as Microsoft Office Word 2003 and Microsoft Office PowerPoint 2003. Because many people are already familiar with these programs, they find Publisher easy to learn. But even if you've never worked with any Microsoft Office program before, great care has gone into making Publisher as intuitive as possible.

In this course, we focus on Publisher's most useful features—the ones most people will use most often and the ones more people would use if they knew how. By the time you finish this Quick Course, you'll have a firm understanding of the components of Publisher, and you'll know enough to experiment on your own with features we don't cover in detail. Specifically, you will know how to:

- Create simple publications
- Develop more complex publications

- Add visual elements
- Design longer publications
- Create custom templates
- Use advanced printing and publishing techniques

Because adequate planning and a basic knowledge of good design are essential for successful publications, we weave these topics into the chapters where appropriate.

In this course, you are asked to assume that you are in charge of creating promotional materials for a company called Adventure Works, which offers tours of the Mojave Desert. Although we focus on how to use Publisher to produce simple but effective publications specifically for Adventure Works, you will easily be able to adapt these examples to your needs. To accomplish its purpose, this course walks you through procedures one step at a time. But we don't take a simple "do this, do that" approach, because when you've finished the course, we want you to be able to apply what you've learned to your own work.

We don't go into detail about installing Publisher on your computer, assuming that the program has already been installed either separately or as part of a Microsoft Office 2003 package. We also assume that you have experience working with Microsoft Windows (98, 2000, Me, XP, or later) and that you know how to start programs, move windows, click commands on menus, highlight text, and so on. If you are new to Windows, we suggest you take a look at the appropriate edition of *Quick Course in Microsoft Windows*, which will help you come up to speed. Finally, we assume you are using a mouse. You can perform many Publisher functions using the keyboard, but a mouse is required for some tasks.

To accomplish its purpose, this course allows you to learn Publisher in an approach that we call *Tell Me, Show Me, Let Me Do It*.

- **Tell Me.** Read through a simple explanation of each function and procedure.

- **Show Me.** The first time you perform a procedure, we explain how you need to set things up and why, what's going on at each step, and what the results will be. And we include lots of screen shots so that you can check your work in progress. The exercises indicate items you should click and keys you should press by showing them in **bold** type. If we want you to press two keys simultaneously, we show the keys one after the other, separated by plus signs—for example, **Ctrl+N**. Anything you should type is shown in *bold italic* type. So there is never any question about what you need to do when.

- **Let Me Do It.** As you learn new skills and increase your proficiency, you work through procedures you have already learned on your own; you can refer back to earlier exercises at any time if you have questions.

The step-by-step instructions in the course tutorial are self-contained, meaning that you create the files you need as you go along, and no additional files are necessary.

With that brief orientation out of the way, let's start learning how to use Publisher!

PART ONE

LEARNING THE BASICS

In Part One, you learn basic techniques for working with simple Publisher documents. In Chapter 1, you begin by creating a promotional postcard, paying close attention to color schemes, text, and the various components that are common to all publications. In Chapter 2, you use a wizard to design a flyer and then learn how to work with frames and how to combine formatting options. Finally, in Chapter 3, you see how to make your publications stand out by adding graphics, fancy text, and other visual enhancements.

CREATING SIMPLE PUBLICATIONS

In this chapter, you jump right in and create your first publication—a promotional postcard for a fictitious business called Adventure Works. You learn the various parts of a publication, how to work with color schemes and text, and how to save and print your work. You can use these simple techniques to design any type of postcard, such as an appointment reminder, an event announcement, or a change of address.

When you have finished this chapter, you will know how to do the following:

- Create your first publication
- Give Publisher instructions
- Save, close, and open publications
- Move around a publication
- Work with text
- Use task panes to make design changes
- Check spelling
- Print publications
- Create other simple publications
- Get help
- Quit Publisher

Select a design
and color scheme
to use for all your
publications.

Adventure Works

Come with us for some
exciting, unforgettable
adventures and fun!

1420 Desert Avenue
Suite 102
Palm Springs, CA 92262

Phone: 800-555-4500
Fax: 760-555-4501
E-mail: tours@adworks.tld
Web: www.adworks.tld

Adventure Works Specialty Tours

Adventure Works offers exciting, educa-
tional tours of the Mojave Desert's diverse
and beautiful natural features such as mountains, lakes, and nature preserves. Call now
for specific tours and price information!

Store often-used
text as a personal
information set.

Customize the
publication by
replacing placeholder
text with your own.

Adventure Works

1420 Desert Avenue
Suite 102
Palm Springs, CA 92262

Phone: 800-555-4500
Fax: 760-555-4501
E-mail: tours@adworks.tld
Web: www.adworks.tld

Sandy Rhodes
President

Quickly convert
an existing publication
to a different type.

CREATING YOUR FIRST PUBLICATION

If you have worked with any of the other Microsoft Office 2003 programs, you'll find that starting Publisher and creating a publication is easy and intuitive. Even if this is the first Office 2003 program you have used, Publisher provides on-screen clues for how to proceed, so you will soon get the hang of things.

To create your first publication, you will select the type of publication—in this case, a postcard—and then customize the template (form document) that Publisher provides. Because most publications include the same sort of information—your name, company name, address, and so on—when you start creating your first publication, you are asked to provide this information so that you have to type it only once.

CHOOSING A PUBLICATION TYPE

It's time to get started, so let's fire up Publisher and start creating a new publication. The first step is to choose a type of publication from among the many categories defined by Publisher. Follow these steps:

1. Click the **Start** button at the left end of the Windows taskbar, click **All Programs**, click **Microsoft Office**, and then click **Microsoft Office Publisher 2003** on the **All Programs** submenu.

DIFFERENT WAYS OF CLICKING

For beginning users, here's a quick recap of mouse terminology. Clicking means pressing and releasing the primary mouse button once. Double-clicking means pressing and releasing the primary mouse button twice in rapid succession. Right-clicking means pressing and releasing the secondary mouse button once. (If you are left-handed and have switched the action of the mouse buttons, use the left button as a right-click button.)

OTHER WAYS TO START PUBLISHER

Instead of starting Publisher from the Start menu, you can create a shortcut icon for Publisher on your desktop. Right-click an open area of the desktop, and on the shortcut menu, click New and then Shortcut. In the Create Shortcut dialog box, click the Browse button, navigate to C:\Program Files\Microsoft Office\OFFICE11\MSPUB.EXE, click OK, and then click Next. Type a name for the shortcut icon, and then click Finish. For maximum efficiency, you can start Publisher and open a recently used publication by clicking the publication on the My Recent Documents submenu of the Start menu, where Windows stores the names of up to 15 of the most recently opened files. For even greater efficiency, you can install a New Office Document and an Open Office Document shortcut to the All Programs menu, which, when clicked, open Publisher and either a new or an existing publication at the same time. If you performed a complete installation of Office, these shortcuts were installed automatically. But even if you performed a typical Office installation, as we did here, you can still go back and run the Office 2003 setup again to add these shortcuts.

If Publisher is the first Office program you use after you install Office 2003, you will be prompted to activate the product before the Publisher window shown in this graphic opens:

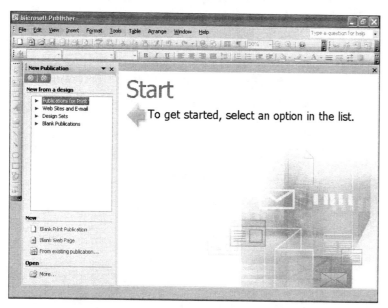

As you can see, the window is divided roughly in two, with the New Publication task pane on the left side of the screen and the main work area on the right. You see the New Publication task pane every time you start Publisher. It has three areas:

- The "New from a design" area contains four options, allowing you to choose a type of publication (such as newsletters, flyers, and business cards); choose from a selection of pre-existing web site and e-mail formats; choose a publication design scheme (called a set) so that you can create a collection of publications that have the same overall look; or choose a blank publication type (such as a page, postcard, or banner) with no formatting or styles applied.

- The New area contains three options, allowing you to create a publication from scratch by implementing a blank publication scheme, to create a new blank web page, or to create a new publication based on an existing one.

DIFFERENT CONFIGURATIONS

The screenshots in this book depict Publisher 2003 installed as part of a Typical installation of Microsoft Office 2003 on a Windows XP computer with an 800-by-600 screen resolution. Our system is set to display file extensions. If you are using a different version of Windows or a different resolution, or have a different setup, you might notice slight differences in the appearance of your screens.

■ The Open area lists publications you have worked on recently, and a More link displays the Open dialog box so that you can quickly locate other files.

2. In the **New from a design** list box, click **Publications for Print**, and then click **Postcards**.

The task pane now lists the types of postcards available, and the main work area displays miniature images (called thumbnails) of postcards, as shown in this graphic:

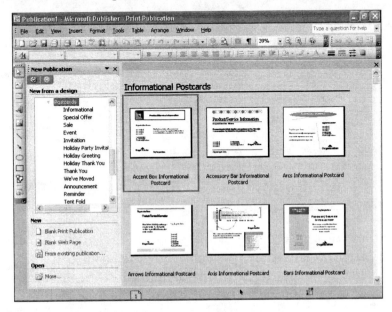

3. If your Windows taskbar is visible across the bottom of the screen and you want your screen to match ours, right-click

USING THE SCROLL BARS

Publisher's window is often not big enough to display all of its contents. To bring out-of-sight information into view, you can use the scroll bars. Clicking the arrow at the end of a scroll bar moves the window's contents a small distance in the direction of the arrow. Clicking on either side of the scroll box in the scroll bar moves the contents one windowful. The position of the scroll box in relation to the scroll bar indicates the position of the window in relation to its contents. For example, if the scroll box is at the top of the vertical scroll bar, you are viewing the top of the page. You can drag the scroll box to see a specific part of the page.

a blank area of the taskbar, click **Properties** on the short-cut menu, select the **Auto-hide the taskbar** check box, and click **OK**.

4. Scroll down the work area on the right until you see the Tilt Informational Postcard thumbnail.

5. Click the **Tilt Informational Postcard** thumbnail once.

   The New Publication task pane is replaced by the Post-card Options task pane. Publisher starts a wizard to collect information that will be used in your publications. You now see the Personal Information dialog box, shown in this graphic:

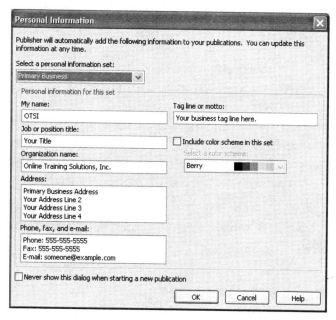

You will fill in the requested information in the next procedure.

FILLING IN YOUR PERSONAL INFORMATION

Publisher saves your personal information for you so that you don't have to re-enter it every time you need to use it in a publication. Follow these steps to fill in your personal information:

1. With **Primary Business** selected in the **Select a personal information set** list, select the text in the My **name** box, and then type *Sandy Rhodes*.

2. In the same manner, replace the entry in the **Job or position title** box with *President*.

SHORTCUT MENUS

Some commands are used only with a specific part of a publication (such as text) or the publication window (such as a toolbar). These commands are grouped together on special menus called shortcut menus. You can display an object's shortcut menu by pointing to the object and clicking the right mouse button. (This action is known as right-clicking; see the tip titled "Different ways of clicking" for more information.)

3. Fill in the remaining boxes with the information shown in this graphic:

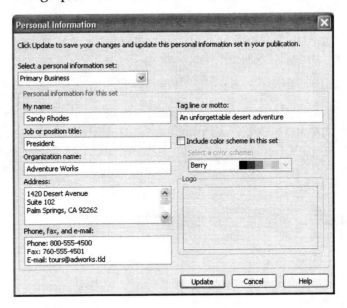

4. You want all the publications you create for Adventure Works to have the same color scheme, so select the **Include color scheme in this set** check box. Then click the **Select a color scheme** down arrow, and click **Desert** in the drop-down list.

5. Click the **Update** button to close the Personal Information dialog box.

OTHER PERSONAL INFORMATION SETS

Publisher can maintain up to four personal information sets: Primary Business, Secondary Business, Other Organization, and Home/Family. For each set, Publisher stores eight items of information. By default, Publisher uses the Primary Business set when you create publications. To apply a different set to a publication, click Personal Information on the Edit menu, select a set from the list box at the top of the Personal Information dialog box, review the information in all the boxes, and click Update. (You also use this command to change an item of information.) To insert a particular item from the active personal information set in a publication, click Personal Information on the Insert menu, and then on the submenu that appears, click the item you want. Publisher inserts the selected item in the publication in its own text box. You can then format the text and text box as needed. (We discuss formatting text and working with text boxes in Chapter 2.) After an item is inserted in a publication, you can add to it or delete parts of it without affecting the way it is stored in the personal information set.

COMPLETING THE PUBLICATION

Having created a personal information set, you can turn your attention back to your new postcard. As you can see, the Postcard Options task pane displays specifications for the postcard's size, second-side information, and copies per sheet. You want the postcard to fit on a quarter page, display only the address on the postcard's reverse side, and print only one copy of the postcard per sheet, so there is not much more to do. Follow these steps:

1. Look over the default options in the task pane's **Size**, **Side 2 information**, and **Copies per sheet** areas.

    The default selections will produce the effect you want.

2. Close the task pane by clicking its **Close** button.

    The work area expands to fill the screen, and the new post-card publication now appears as shown in this graphic:

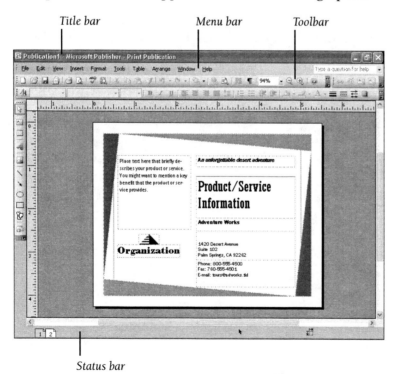

Title bar   *Menu bar*   *Toolbar*

Status bar

Taking up most of the Publisher window is your new post-card, parts of which have been customized with the information from your personal information set. Like most Windows programs, the Publisher window includes the familiar title bar at the top and status bar at the bottom. You also see a menu bar and toolbars, which you use to give Publisher instructions. Although the menu bar and toolbars look the same as those in all Windows programs, they work a little differently, so we'll take a break from our postcard creation to explore them in the next topic.

GIVING PUBLISHER INSTRUCTIONS

We'll pause a moment in the design of the new postcard to introduce some of the ways in which you can give Publisher instructions by using your mouse and keyboard.

USING THE TOOLBARS

One way to give Publisher an instruction is by clicking a toolbar button. This produces the same effect as clicking the corresponding menu command, and then if necessary, clicking OK to accept all the default settings in the command's dialog box. (We'll take a look at menu commands in a moment.)

By default, Publisher arranges its buttons on four toolbars: the Standard, Formatting, and Connect Text Boxes toolbars above the work area; and the Objects toolbar down the left side of the screen. These toolbars all display the same buttons no matter what task you are carrying out, but buttons representing commands that are not available are dimmed, as you can see on the Formatting toolbar when no postcard element is selected. Try this:

1. Point to each button on the Formatting toolbar.

   Even when a button is dimmed, pointing to the button displays a box called a *ScreenTip* containing the button's name, as shown in this graphic:

2. Click anywhere in the words **Product/Service Information**.

   Publisher surrounds the text box that contains the words with small white circles called *handles* to indicate that the text box is selected. The Formatting toolbar's buttons now become active, as shown in this graphic:

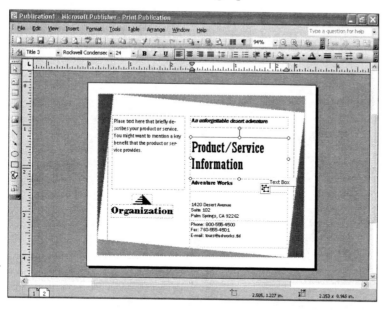

3. Click the pyramid graphic above the word *Organization*. (If the Picture toolbar appears when you click the pyramid graphic, click the toolbar's **Close** button to close it.)

With the graphic selected, the Formatting toolbar's text-related buttons are dimmed, but the buttons that relate to formatting graphics remain active.

REPOSITIONING A TOOLBAR

Each toolbar has a move handle at its left or top end. You can drag this handle to change the location of the toolbar on the screen. Follow these steps to reposition the Formatting toolbar:

1. Point to the Formatting toolbar's move handle. When the pointer changes to a four-headed arrow, drag the toolbar down over the work area.

The toolbar reshapes itself as a separate "floating" object with a title bar and a Close button, as shown in this graphic:

2. Double-click the toolbar's title bar to "dock" it at the top of the work area again.

3. Drag the toolbar's move handle up and to the right until the Formatting toolbar appears on the same row as the Standard and Connect Text Boxes toolbars.

The top of your screen now looks similar to the one in this graphic:

Move handle   *Toolbar Options button*

Publisher hides the buttons that you are less likely to use and adds a Toolbar Options button at the right end of each toolbar so that you can access the hidden buttons. But suppose you want to see more of the Formatting toolbar's buttons and don't mind seeing fewer of the Standard toolbar's buttons. Try this:

4. Drag the Formatting toolbar's move handle to the left as far as you can.

5. Click the Standard toolbar's **Toolbar Options** button.

You now see a palette of all the hidden buttons on the Standard and Formatting toolbars, as shown in this graphic:

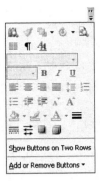

DOCKING ELSEWHERE

You can dock a toolbar along any of the four sides of the program window simply by dragging it there. (Drag a docked toolbar by its move handle or a floating toolbar by its title bar.) If you drag a docked toolbar over the work area and then double-click the floating toolbar's title bar to redock it, the toolbar automatically returns to its previously docked location.

6. The postcard is small enough to fit in the work area, so drag the Formatting toolbar back to its original location below the Standard and Connect Text Boxes toolbars.

Most of the buttons on all three bars are now displayed.

GIVING MENU COMMANDS

In Publisher, you use standard Windows techniques to click a command on a menu or submenu and to work with dialog boxes. Like other Office 2003 programs, Publisher initially displays a subset of the available commands and then adjusts the menus as you work so that they display the commands you use most often. As a quick example, let's take a look at the View menu:

1. Click **View** on the menu bar to drop down the View menu.

   The chevron (the double arrowheads) at the bottom of the menu indicates that one or more commands are hidden because they are not the ones most commonly used.

2. Continue pointing to the word *View*. (You can also click the chevron to make hidden commands appear.)

   The chevron disappears, and the menu expands to display more commands, as shown in this graphic:

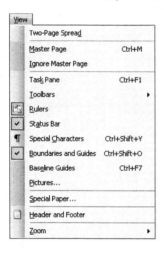

   The status of a less frequently used command is indicated by a darker shade of blue to the left of the menu command. If you click one of the dark blue commands, in the future it will appear with the same color as other commands and will no longer be hidden.

3. Click **Rulers**.

   The rulers above and to the left of the work area disappear.

4. Move the pointer along the menu bar, pausing to drop down each menu in turn.

   Notice that when one menu is expanded, they all expand.

PERSONALIZED MENUS

Publisher's menus adjust themselves to the way you work, making more commands available as you use them. Commands you don't use are hidden so that they don't get in the way. As a result, your menus might not look exactly like the ones shown in the screenshots in this course, and occasionally we might tell you to click a command that is not visible. When this happens, don't panic. Click the menu name, and wait until the menu expands so that all its commands are displayed.

KEYBOARD SHORTCUTS

Publisher provides many keyboard shortcuts for working with publications. If a command has such a shortcut, it is displayed to the right of the command on the menu. Shortcuts are also available for moving around, applying formatting, and other common tasks. Unfortunately, the list of shortcuts is too lengthy to reproduce here. If you know the keyboard shortcuts of other Office programs, such as Word, you can use many of them in Publisher. If you are not familiar with these shortcuts, type "keyboard short-cuts" in the "Type a question for help" box at the right end of the menu bar, and press Enter.

SAVING, CLOSING, AND OPENING PUBLICATIONS

After you've created a publication, you'll want to save it so that you can step away from it or even close it, and then come back to it later to find the information in the publication just as you left it.

SAVING A PUBLICATION

To save a new publication, you can click the Save button on the Standard toolbar or click either Save or Save As on the File menu. You can then specify the publication's name and storage location. Follow these steps:

1. On the **File** menu, click **Save As**.

    Publisher displays the Save As dialog box, as shown in this graphic:

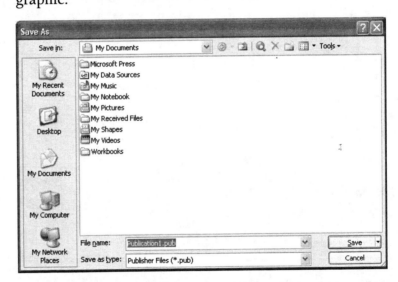

SAVING OPTIONS

By default, publications are saved in the Publisher Files format, and templates are saved in the Publisher Template format. To save a file in a different format, in the Save As dialog box, click the "Save as type" down arrow, and in the drop-down list, select the format you need. If you want to keep a backup copy of your work, click the down arrow in the Save As dialog box, and then in the drop-down list, click "Save with Backup." The backup file will be called Backup of [*File name*] and will be saved in the same folder as the current file.

2. With *Publication1.pub* highlighted in the **File name** box, type *Postcard* to replace Publisher's suggested name.

3. Be sure that the **My Documents** folder appears in the **Save in** box and, leaving the other settings in the dialog box as they are, click **Save**.

    When you return to the publication, notice that *Postcard* has replaced *Publication1* in the title bar.

    From now on, you can click the Save button or click Save on the File menu any time you want to quickly save changes to this file. Publisher already knows the name of this file, so instead of asking you to name the file, it simply over-writes the previous version with the new version. If you want to save your changes but preserve the previous version, you can assign a different name to the new version by clicking Save As on the File menu, entering the new name in the "File name" box, and clicking Save.

CLOSING AND OPENING A PUBLICATION

Now that you've saved the postcard so that its information is stored, you can get some practice in closing its file and then opening it again. Let's get going:

1. On the **File** menu, click **Close**.

    The Postcard publication disappears from view, and the New Publication task pane and start window takes its place.

2. On the Standard toolbar, click the **Open** button.

    The Open Publication dialog box appears, as shown in this graphic:

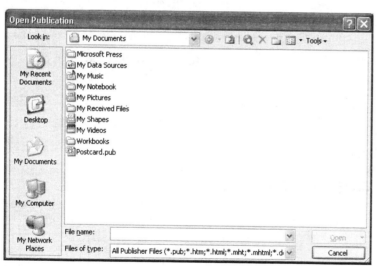

SAVING IN A DIFFERENT FOLDER

To store a file in a folder other than the default folder, in the Save As dialog box, click the "Save in" down arrow, and use the drop-down list to find the folder in which you want to save the file. Double-click that folder, and then click Save. You can also click the icons on the shortcuts bar along the left side of the Save As dialog box to quickly move to common folders and recent files. To create a new folder in which to save a file, click the Create New Folder button at the top of the Save As dialog box before you save the file, and then name the new folder. To change the default folder to something other than the My Documents folder, click Options on the Tools menu, click the General tab, and in the "File locations" area, click the Modify button to select a new location in the Modify Location dialog box. Click OK twice when you are finished.

3. In the Open Publication dialog box, double-click the **Post-card** icon.

4. If the Load Fonts dialog box appears, follow the font sub-stitution instructions in the dialog box, and click **OK**.

    If your computer doesn't have some of the fonts used in the publication you want to open, Publisher automatically sub-stitutes the closest matching fonts. Publisher then opens the Postcard publication, which replaces the start window on your screen.

MOVING AROUND A PUBLICATION

You need to know how to move around a publication for two reasons: so that you can view parts of a publication that don't fit in the window, and so that you can edit its text.

MOVING TO A DIFFERENT PAGE

If a page of a publication is bigger than the window, you can bring hidden parts into view by using the scroll bars. If you want to display a specific page of a publication, you can use the page controls in the status bar. Let's try out these controls now:

1. Click the page control labeled 2 on the status bar.

INFORMATION ABOUT
Scroll bars, page 6

**OTHER WAYS TO OPEN
A PUBLICATION**

In addition to clicking the Open button, you can also display the Open Publication dialog box by either clicking Open on the File menu or pressing Ctrl+O. To open a recently used publication, you can click its name at the bottom of the File menu or in the Open area at the bottom of the New Publication task pane. If Pub-lisher is not already open, you can open a recently saved publication quickly by clicking the Start button on the Windows taskbar, clicking My Recent Documents, and then clicking the name of the publication you want to open.

**OPTIONS AVAILABLE IN THE
OPEN DIALOG BOX**

You can use the "Look in" box in the Open Publication dialog box to navigate to the folder containing the publication you want to open, and you can also click icons on the My Places bar on the left side of the dialog box to display the contents of specific folders in which you might have saved the publication. You can change the way the list is displayed by clicking the Views down arrow. Clicking Preview splits the list pane so that a preview of the file selected on the left is displayed on the right, allowing you to check visually that you are opening the publication you want. You can click the Tools button to search for, delete, or rename files; to add a publication to your list of favorites on the My Places bar; and to provide ready access to a computer on a network by mapping its hard disk so that it shows up as a drive letter on your computer. Finally, you can click the Open down arrow to open the selected file as read-only, meaning that you can view it but not change it; or to open the selected file in an Internet browser window.

Publisher displays page 2 of the publication, which, as you can see here, is the back of the postcard:

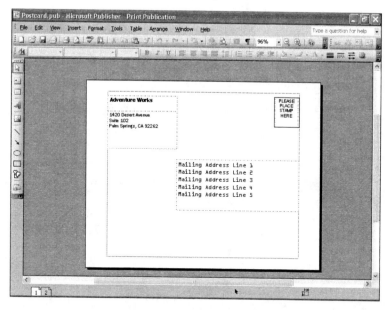

2. On the **Edit** menu, click **Go to Page**.

   You can also press Ctrl+G to open this dialog box. The Go To Page dialog box appears, as shown in this graphic:

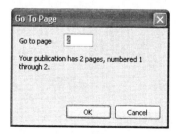

3. Replace the 2 in the box with *1*, and click **OK** to return to page 1 of the publication.

   This command is most useful when your publication has numerous pages.

ZOOMING IN AND OUT

In addition to scrolling through a large page and moving to different pages of a multi-page publication, you might also want to zoom in for a closer look at a particular element or zoom out to get an overview of an entire page. With Publisher, you can zoom in and out in several ways. Before you start working on the text of the postcard, let's experiment with zooming.

1. On the Standard toolbar, click the **Zoom** down arrow to display a drop-down list of standard zoom percentages.

   Also included in the list is the Whole Page option, which displays the entire page on one screen, and the Page Width option, which expands the publication so that its width fills the work area. If an object is selected on the page, Publisher adds a Selected Objects option, which zooms the window to the percentage that allows full viewing of that object.

2. Click **200%** to zoom in on the postcard.

   The postcard is now magnified, as shown in this graphic:

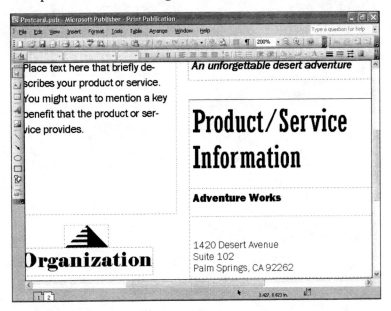

3. On the **View** menu, click **Zoom** to display a list of zoom options as a submenu, and then change the zoom percentage to **100%**.

   When you want to quickly switch between the current view and the actual size view (100%), you can press the F9 key.

4. To zoom to the next lowest percentage, click the **Zoom Out** button on the Standard toolbar.

   Publisher switches the view to 75%.

5. Click the **Zoom In** button to return to 100%.

IDENTIFYING PARTS OF A PUBLICATION

As you move the mouse pointer over the postcard now on your screen, you might notice ScreenTips popping up to identify its different parts. (Remember that you experimented with the ScreenTips feature earlier in "Using the Toolbars.") Try this:

1. Move the pointer over the words *Adventure Works*, and pause for a moment.

   Publisher displays a ScreenTip containing the words *Organization Name Text Box*.

2. Now move the pointer over the pyramid graphic above the word *Organization*, and pause.

   The ScreenTip identifies this part of the postcard as *Logo Picture*. If you were to move the pointer below the pyramid to the word *Organization*, you would see a ScreenTip identifying the text as *Logo Text*. If you have trouble getting the ScreenTips to appear, be patient, and be sure to pause over each item.

WORKING WITH TEXT

Unlike text in a word-processing program, text in Publisher must be contained in a text box. Publisher refers to all the text in a single text box as a story. (We discuss more about working with text boxes in Chapter 2.) As you can see, the postcard template has several text boxes. Some of them contain placeholder text, meaning that Publisher has used dummy text to show you what to place where. In this topic, we show you how to work with the text in order to customize the postcard with your own words.

ADDING AND REPLACING TEXT

You need to select the placeholder text in order to replace it. The simplest way to learn how to select text is to actually do it, so let's get going:

1. Click anywhere in the **Product/Service Information** placeholder. Then if you see a "bubble," called a *tippage*, telling you that you can press Ctrl+A to select all the text in a story, press **Esc** to close it.

   Publisher highlights all the text in the text box by changing it to white on black to indicate that it is selected. Publisher

TIPPAGES

Tippages are yellow "bubbles" that occasionally pop up to offer advice on more efficient ways to carry out specific tasks. To remove a tippage from the screen, click it or press Esc. If you find this feature a nuisance, you can turn it off. Click Options on the Tools menu, click the User Assistance tab, deselect the "Show tippages" check box, and click OK. To reset tippages so that ones you have seen before reappear under similar circumstances, click the Reset Tips button.

INFORMATION ABOUT
Lines, page 59
Grouping objects, page 103

also displays an Ungroup Objects button below the selected text box. Although you may not be able to see it very well, the text box has a solid line above it, and the text box and line have been grouped so that if you move, size, or delete one, the other will be moved, sized, or deleted as well.

2. With the text selected, type *Mojave Desert Jeep Toors*, being sure to misspell *Tours*, and press the **Spacebar**.

   Publisher underlines the misspelling with a red, wavy line to draw the error to your attention.

3. Click anywhere in the **Place text here…** placeholder to select both the text and its text box, and then type the following paragraph (including the spelling errors, which appear in regular type):

   Adventure Works offers jeep toors *of the Mojave Desert, including the most remote and* seanic *locations. Tours range from $45 to $610 per person. Our jeeps are safe and* comfterble. *Call now to book* you're *tour!*

INFORMATION ABOUT
Correcting mistakes, page 30
Checking spelling, page 27

   Notice that Publisher automatically corrects the misspelling *comfterble* to *comfortable* using a feature called Auto-Correct. However, AutoCorrect cannot detect the correct spellings for all incorrect words, so it underlines the other misspellings with a red, wavy line. You will deal with the errors later in this chapter.

4. On the Standard toolbar, click the **Save** button to save your work.

USING AUTOCORRECT

As you enter text in a text box, Publisher's AutoCorrect feature corrects common typos. You have already seen how AutoCorrect handled the word *comfortable*. As another example, AutoCorrect will replace *teh* with *the*. AutoCorrect also corrects two initial capital letters, such as *ADventure*, and capitalizes the names of days. To include your own commonly misspelled entries in AutoCorrect, click AutoCorrect Options on the Tools menu. When the AutoCorrect dialog box appears, type the misspelling in the Replace box, type the correct spelling in the With box, and then click Add to add the new entry to AutoCorrect's list of common misspellings. To delete entries from AutoCorrect's list, select the entry and click the Delete button. To turn AutoCorrect off, in the AutoCorrect dialog box, deselect the "Replace text as you type" check box. When you have finished making changes in this dialog box, click OK.

EDITING PERSONAL INFORMATION

Publisher has drawn from your personal information set to fill in some of the postcard text. Let's adjust some of the text it has added:

1. In the tag-line text box in the upper-right corner, double-click **An** to select the word and the following space. Then type *Come with use for an*.

    If you have trouble seeing the text, remember that you can change the zoom magnification. As the words you type fill the text box, Publisher automatically adjusts the text size to make it fit. Why? Because a formatting feature called *automatic copyfitting* has been applied to this text box so that the tag line will always be a single line.

2. To add a new line of text to the Phone/Fax/E-mail text box in the lower-right corner, click an insertion point at the end of the e-mail address, and press **Enter**. Then type *Web: www.adworks.tld*.

    The results are shown in this graphic:

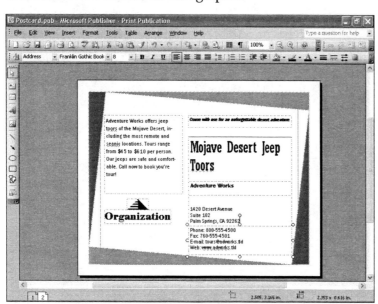

INFORMATION ABOUT
Zooming, page 17
Automatic copyfitting, page 47

DELETING A PLACEHOLDER TEXT BOX

Sometimes you will want to delete a placeholder text box rather than replacing its text. (Always delete placeholders if you're not going to use them; otherwise, they appear just as they are when you print the final publication.) If you want to delete the text but leave the text box, you can select the text and press the

WHOLE WORD SELECTION
By default, Publisher selects whole words. For example, if you start a selection in the middle of a word and then drag beyond the last character, Publisher selects the entire word. You can tell Publisher to select only the characters you drag across. Click Options on the Tools menu, and on the Edit tab, deselect the "When selecting, automatically select entire word" check box. Then click OK.

INFORMATION ABOUT
Creating a logo, page 80

Delete key. If you want to delete the text box as well as the text it contains, you must use another method. To demonstrate, let's delete the Logo placeholder text box on the left side of the postcard:

1. In the **Logo** placeholder, select **Organization**.

   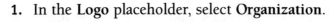

   Because a wizard is associated with the logo, a Wizard button appears below the text box. You can ignore it for now.

2. With the Logo placeholder text box selected, click **Delete Object** on the **Edit** menu.

   The logo and its accompanying text disappear.

3. Click the **Save** button to save the postcard.

MOVING AND COPYING TEXT

Like most Windows programs, Publisher provides two methods for moving text. The first method involves cutting and pasting, which is useful for moving text from one page to another or even from one publication to another. The second method involves dragging and dropping, which is useful for moving text to a different location on the same page. Similarly, two methods are provided for copying text. Let's experiment:

INFORMATION ABOUT
Copying between publications, page 46

1. Drag across the sentence that begins **Our jeeps** to select it.

   You can also click an insertion point to the left of the *O*, hold down the Shift key, and press the Arrow keys until the sentence is selected. Make sure to include the space following the sentence in your selection.

2. On the Standard toolbar, click the **Cut** button.

KEYBOARD MOVING/COPYING

Being able to move and copy by pressing keys is handy if you already have your fingers on the keyboard and you don't want to stop to use the mouse. To use a keyboard shortcut to move text, select the text and press Ctrl+X. Then to paste it, click an insertion point where you want the text to appear and press Ctrl+V. To copy text instead of moving it, follow the same procedure but use Ctrl+C instead of Ctrl+X.

USING WORD TO EDIT TEXT

Publisher 2003 is very similar to Word 2003 in its text editing techniques and capabilities. If you installed Publisher as part of the Office 2003 Suite, you have Word installed on your computer, and you can use that program to edit your text. This ability to move text between the two programs is handy if you want to produce longer publications, or if you simply prefer to use Word for text editing. To edit text in Word, select the text box that contains the text you want to edit, right-click the text box, and on the shortcut menu, click Change Text and then Edit Story in Microsoft Word. Word opens with the text displayed in a document window. When you finish editing the text, you can exit Word and update the Publisher file by clicking the Close & Return to [*Publication name*] command on Word's File menu.

Publisher removes the text from the publication and stores it in a temporary storage place in your computer's memory, called the *Clipboard*. If you want to copy text instead of moving it, click the **Copy** button.

3. Click an insertion point to the left of the *T* in *Tours*, and on the Standard toolbar, click the **Paste** button.

Publisher inserts the cut text, following it with a space.

4. Select the word **remote**, and click the **Cut** button.

5. Click an insertion point to the left of the *s* in *seanic*, and click the **Paste** button.

6. Double-click the word **seanic**.

7. Hold down the left mouse button, drag the selection to the left of the *a* in *and*, and then release the button.

Publisher moves the word to its new location, adjusting the spaces appropriately. The words *remote* and *seanic* have now switched places. (If you want to copy text using drag-and-drop editing instead of moving it, hold down the Ctrl key while dragging the selection.)

UNDOING AND REDOING COMMANDS

For those occasions when you make a mistake or have second thoughts about a change you have made, Publisher provides a safety net: the Undo command. If you undo a change and then decide you were right the first time, you can use the Redo command to reinstate the change. Follow the steps on the next page to use these commands.

THE OFFICE CLIPBOARD

The Office Clipboard temporarily stores cut or copied data from all Office programs. Because the Clipboard is a temporary storage place, turning off your computer erases any information stored there. You can use the Clipboard to transfer data from one file to another in the same program or from one program to another.

To display the Clipboard task pane, click Office Clipboard on the Edit menu. Each item you cut or copy is represented in the Clipboard task pane by the icon of the program in which it was created, as well as the first few characters of text or a thumbnail image. To paste one item, click an insertion point in the desired location, and then in the Clipboard task pane, click the item you want to paste. To delete an item from the task pane, hold the pointer over the item, click the down arrow that appears, and then click Delete in the drop-down list. To paste all of the Clipboard items at once, click the Paste All button at the top of the task pane. To clear all of the items from the task pane, click the Clear All button. To change when and where the Clipboard task pane is displayed, click the Options button at the bottom of the task pane and then click the command you want. To close the task pane, click its Close button.

1. You're not sure you like the words in their new order, so click the **Undo** button.

    Publisher reverses the drag operation from the previous procedure.

2. Change your mind again, and click the **Redo** button to move *seanic* back before *and*. Then click a blank area of the screen.

    With all the text in place, the postcard now looks like this graphic:

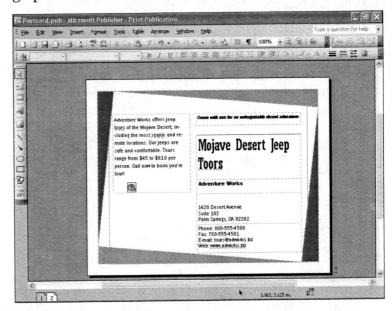

MORE ABOUT UNDO AND REDO

To the right of both the Undo and Redo buttons is a down arrow that you can click to display a list of the last actions you performed, including text entry, text and graphics formatting, graphics changes, and other tasks. (The list can display a maximum of 12 previous actions.) When you click any of these actions, you will undo or redo not only the action you clicked, but all actions you did afterward, so use this feature with discretion. Another way to undo and redo edits is to click the Undo *[Action]* and Redo *[Action]* commands on the Edit menu. You can also press Ctrl+Z to undo an action, and Ctrl+Y to redo something you just undid.

USING TASK PANES TO MAKE DESIGN CHANGES

You've seen how to simplify the task of creating a publication by using one of Publisher's wizards. Obviously, adding text is easier when the text boxes for all the elements are already in place. But what if you decide you don't like the design or color scheme you chose? Do you have to start all over again?

No—in fact, it's easy to change your publication's design. You simply use options in the Publication Designs and Color Schemes task panes. In this topic, we work with those task panes to really make your postcard shine.

CHANGING THE BASIC DESIGN

Suppose you've decided that the Tilt design doesn't quite fit the image you want for Adventure Works. Let's open a task pane and look for something more appropriate:

1. With the postcard displayed on your screen, click **Task Pane** on the **View** menu.

2. Click the down arrow on the task pane's title bar, and then click **Publication Designs** in the drop-down list.

   The Publication Designs task pane appears to the left of the postcard, as shown in this graphic:

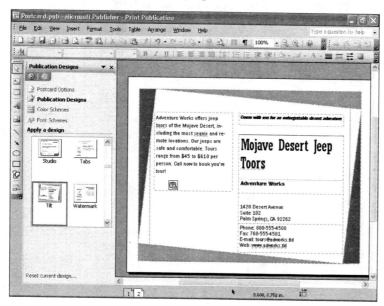

   If necessary, scroll the postcard into view as we've done.

3. In the **Apply a design** area, scroll through the design thumbnails so that you can get a feel for all the designs that are available for a postcard publication. When you have finished browsing, click the **Blocks** thumbnail.

   Note the results in the pane on the right. The design has changed, but the color scheme remains intact.

4. The Blocks design doesn't really fit the tone you want for a company providing a service to tourists, so experiment with some of the other design templates.

RESETTING A DESIGN

If you don't like a change you have made to a design, you can restore the original settings. First, display the Publication Designs task pane for the open publication and then click the "Reset current design" link in the bottom part of the task pane. Publisher displays the Reset Design dialog box, in which you can select check boxes to reset the original formatting of text and objects, restore deleted objects and pages, and reestablish the original page setup and layout. You can also remove objects and pages you have added and restore text and pictures you have changed. To reset all of the design changes you've made for the publication, select the "All of the above" check box. Click OK when you have finished.

5. When you have finished experimenting, point to the first **Waves** thumbnail in the **Apply a design** area, pause to ensure that its associated ScreenTip reads *Waves Informational Postcard*, and then click this **Waves** design.

If you click a Waves design other than *Waves Informational Postcard*, Publisher might delete some of the information on the postcard to accommodate the design type. For the design you just chose, Publisher has to adjust some text box sizes so that the text will fit. If it could not adjust the text boxes sufficiently, Publisher would display a Text in Overflow indicator at the bottom of the text box to warn you that some of the text is hidden in an overflow area.

The results are shown in this graphic:

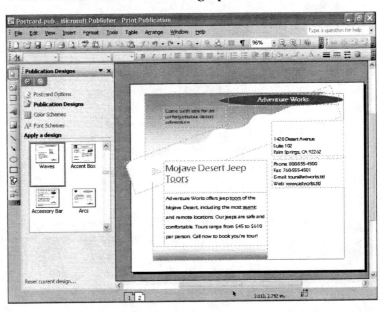

CHANGING THE COLOR SCHEME

If you are going to print your publication in color, you need to carefully consider its color scheme. Choosing colors that are appropriate for the message you want to send is extremely important. If you understand how colors work together and how they affect your audience, you will probably have no trouble devising your own color schemes. The rest of us can be thankful that Publisher provides a number of preset color schemes to choose from.

Although the Desert color scheme seemed appropriate when you chose it earlier, the heavy brown theme doesn't suit a fun tourist activity. Let's use the Color Schemes task pane to find a livelier scheme:

1. In the upper area of the task pane, click **Color Schemes** to display the **Color Schemes** task pane.

2. Scroll through the **Apply a color scheme** list, and select any color schemes that catch your eye, noting their effects on the postcard in the work pane on the right.

3. When you have finished experimenting, click **Tropics**.

4. Click the task pane's **Close** button to close the task pane and get a better look at the postcard's new colors.

    The Tropics scheme includes colors you might associate with the desert, but the overall color scheme is more vibrant than Desert.

5. Save your work.

CHECKING SPELLING

Now that you have entered the postcard's text and finalized its design and color scheme, you're ready to print, right? Not quite. Before printing any publication, you should always check it for spelling and grammatical errors. As you added the text, you deliberately included a few misspellings, and Publisher flagged most of them with red, wavy underlines. This feature, called *check spelling as you type*, alerts you to errors as you work.

CHECKING THE SPELLING OF ONE WORD

Let's fix one of the misspelled words now:

1. Right-click the word **Toors** in the postcard's title text (the text that begins with *Mojave Desert*).

    Publisher checks the underlined word against its built-in dictionary and displays the shortcut menu shown on the following page.

SPELLING OPTIONS

As you have seen, Publisher flags any misspellings you type with red, wavy underlines. It also flags duplicate words, such as *the the*, and words in all capital letters. If you don't want Publisher to flag these items, click Spelling and then Spelling Options on the Tools menu to display the Spelling Options dialog box. Then select or deselect the options you want, and click OK.

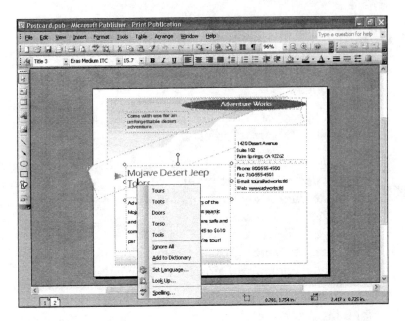

At the top of the shortcut menu, Publisher displays any words in its dictionary that resemble the misspelled word. You can replace the underlined word with one of Publisher's suggestions, ignore the misspelling, add the underlined word to Publisher's dictionary so that the program will recognize the word in the future, change the default language used to check spelling, or open the Check Spelling dialog box for more options.

2. On the shortcut menu, click **Tours** to replace the word with its correct spelling.

CHECKING THE SPELLING OF AN ENTIRE PUBLICATION

If you don't want to stop writing to correct errors, you can check the spelling of an entire publication after you have entered all the text. Follow these steps:

1. With the insertion point still in the title text box, click the **Spelling** button on the Standard toolbar.

A dialog box alerting you that Publisher has finished checking the spelling of the current story appears, as shown in this graphic:

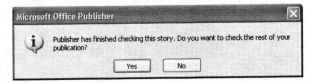

2. Click **Yes** to close the dialog box and continue checking the spelling in the rest of the publication.

    Publisher checks each word in all of the postcard's text boxes against its built-in dictionary, starting with the word containing the insertion point. When it finds a word that is not in its dictionary, Publisher highlights the word and displays the Check Spelling dialog box, as shown in this graphic:

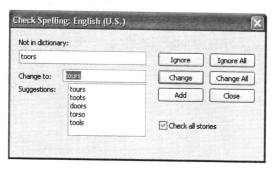

    Possible alternatives for *toors* appear in the Suggestions list, with the closest match to the unrecognized word displayed in the "Change to" box. (Notice that Publisher's suggestions have the same capitalization as the misspelled word.) The "Check all stories" check box is selected by default, telling Publisher to check the spelling of all the words that appear in the postcard.

3. To correct the current misspelling, verify that *tours* appears in the **Change to** box. (Click it in the **Suggestions** list if it doesn't.) Then click **Change** to correct this misspelling.

    Publisher then stops at *seanic*.

CHECKING SPELLING IN OTHER LANGUAGES

You can use supplemental dictionaries of other languages or of special terms, such as medical or legal dictionaries, to check the spelling of your publications. After you have installed a special dictionary, you select text in a publication and designate it as written in another language by clicking Language and then Set Language on the Tools menu. Select the language you want in the "Mark selected text as" list, and then click OK. Then you're ready to check the spelling of the publication in that language.

DICTIONARIES IN PUBLISHER

Publisher checks your spelling by comparing each word in the publication with those in both its built-in dictionary and its supplemental dictionary, which is called *Custom.dic*. You cannot change the built-in dictionary, but you can add words to Custom.dic by clicking the Add button in the Check Spelling dialog box.

4. In the **Suggestions** list, click **scenic**, and then click **Change**.

The next problem Publisher identifies is the web address for Adventure Works. Although this address is not in either of Publisher's dictionaries, it is correct.

INFORMATION ABOUT
Dictionaries, page 29

5. Click **Add** to add the address to Publisher's supplemental dictionary.

You'll notice that Publisher does not flag the e-mail address as a misspelling because it contains the @ character. When Publisher reaches the end of the publication, it closes the Check Spelling dialog box and displays a message stating that the spelling check is complete.

6. Click **OK** to return to the postcard, and then save the publication.

You can't rely on Publisher's spelling checker to identify every error in your publications, because errors of syntax or improper word usage can easily slip by. The postcard contains two errors of this type—*use* should be *us* in the tag line text beginning with *Come with us*; and *you're* should be *your* in the last sentence of the descriptive text (which you can't see because the text overflows its text box).

7. Select the text box, point to one of its move handles (the small white circles), and when the pointer changes to a double-headed arrow, drag until you can see all of the text in the text box.

8. In the tag line text, change **use** to *us*.

9. Change **you're** to *your*, and save the publication again.

PRINTING PUBLICATIONS

After you have created and edited a publication, you will most likely want to print it. If you can print from any other Windows program, you should have no trouble printing from Publisher.

SETTING UP FOR PRINTING

When Windows was installed on your computer, the setup program also installed the driver (the control program) for the printer attached to your computer. If you have access to other printers, you can install their drivers by using the Add Printer Wizard in the Printers folder. In Windows XP, you can access this wizard by clicking Printers and Faxes on the Start menu, and then clicking the "Add a printer" link in the Printer Tasks area of the Printers and Faxes window. To access this wizard in versions of Windows earlier than Windows XP, click Settings and then Printers on the Start menu.

To print the entire postcard with all the default settings, you can simply click the Print button on the Standard toolbar. If you want to change any of the settings—for example, if you want to print more than one copy or change which printer Publisher will use—you need to click Print on the File menu to display the Print dialog box. Follow these steps to print the finished postcard:

1. On the **File** menu, click **Print**.

    Publisher displays the dialog box shown in this graphic:

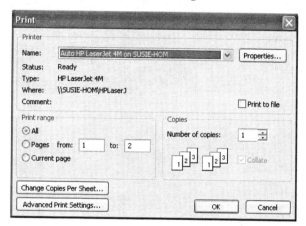

Publisher can access all the installed printers, but only one at a time. To switch printers, click Print on the File menu, click the Name down arrow in the Printer area of the Print dialog box, select the printer you want to use, and then click OK. To change the default printer used for your publications, click Page Setup on the File menu, and change the printer name on the "Printer and Paper" tab of the Page Setup dialog box.

2. In the **Copies** area of the Print dialog box, replace 1 in the **Number of copies** box with 2.

3. Click **OK** to send the file to the printer.

CREATING OTHER SIMPLE PUBLICATIONS

We've shown you how to create a postcard, which is only one of the many types of publications you can create with Publisher. Now you'll learn how to quickly create another postcard using the information you entered for the first one. You'll also see how to create a different type of publication, and how to adjust its text so that it looks just right.

MORE PRINT OPTIONS

If you don't want Publisher to collate multiple copies of multi-page publications, in the Print dialog box, deselect the Collate check box. To print only the page containing the insertion point, click the "Current page" option. To print selected pages, click the Pages option and then enter the page numbers in the "from" and "to" boxes. (For example, enter 2 in the "from" box and 4 in the "to" box to print pages 2, 3, and 4.) Select the "Print to file" check box to "print" an image of the publication to a file on disk. Clicking the Properties button displays a tabbed dialog box with still more printing options, including the ability to switch the page orientation between Portrait (vertical) and Landscape (horizontal).

CREATING A NEW PUBLICATION FROM AN EXISTING ONE

Now we'll introduce you to a way in which you can create a new publication from one you've already created. We'll use the postcard you created as a basis for a second, more general advertising postcard for Adventure Works, so that you don't have to create one from scratch. Try this:

1. Save the postcard, and then on the **File** menu, click **Close** to close the Postcard file.

2. If necessary, on the **View** menu, click **Task Pane** to display the **New Publication** task pane.

3. In the **New** area, click the **From existing publication** link.

    Publisher displays the Create New from Existing Publication dialog box shown in this graphic:

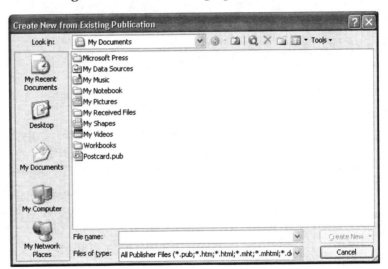

4. Double-click **Postcard**.

    Publisher closes the task pane and opens a copy of the Mojave Desert Jeep Tours postcard as a new unsaved publication.

5. Save the new postcard with the name *General Postcard*.

6. Display the **Color Schemes** task pane by clicking **Color Schemes** on the **Format** menu, change the color scheme to **Crocus**, and then close the task pane.

7. Change the postcard's information to match the text shown in this graphic:

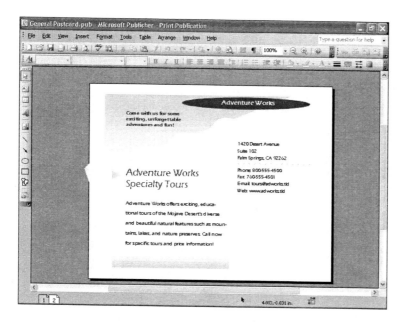

We've changed the magnification for easier readability. To see how the publication would look without the dotted lines around the text boxes, click View, and in the drop-down menu, deselect Boundaries and Guides.

8. Save your changes when you are finished.

DESIGNING A BUSINESS CARD

Let's design a business card for Adventure Works:

1. On the **File** menu, click **Close** to close the Postcard file and display the **New Publication** task pane.

2. In the **New from a design** area, click **Publications for Print**, click **Business Cards**, scroll to the **Waves Business Card** in the work area, and then click it.

   The new business card is displayed in the work area, and the New Publication task pane changes to the Business Card Options task pane. Notice that Publisher has already entered the Adventure Works company name, as well as the name, title, company name, address, and phone information that you provided for your personal information set.

3. In the **Business Card Options** task pane's **Logo** area, click **None** to remove the placeholder logo, and leave the other two options as they are.

4. Click the **Color Schemes** link, and in the **Apply a color scheme** area of the **Color Schemes** task pane, click **Tropics**.

INFORMATION ABOUT
Personal information set, page 7

5. On the **File** menu, click **Save As**, and save the file in the My Documents folder with the name *Business Card*.

6. Close the task pane to expand the work area.

MAKING ADJUSTMENTS TO THE BUSINESS CARD

Right away, you'll notice that your new business card needs some adjustments. For one thing, the web address does not show up in the Phone/Fax/E-mail text box because you entered it manually in the postcard. You need to enter it in the business card, too. Also, Publisher displays the Text in Overflow indicator at the bottom of the phone number text box to warn you that not all the text in this story will fit in the text box (you may need to select the text box to see the indicator). You need to resize the text box to display the phone number and e-mail address, and you need to change the font size to make room for the web address you are about to add. Let's get going:

1. Click the text box to activate it, point to the upper-center handle (be sure to point to the white circle, and not the green one above it), and when the pointer changes to a double-headed resize arrow, drag downward until the text box's upper edge is just above the phone number text.

   The effect you are looking for is shown in this graphic:

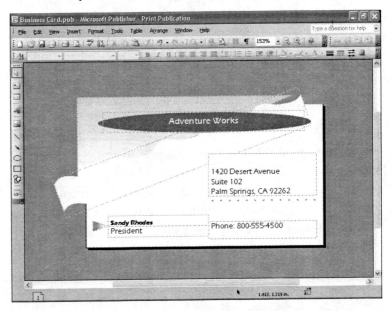

2. Point to the text box's lower-center handle, and when the pointer changes to a double-headed resize arrow, drag downward until you can see the fax number and e-mail address.

The text box now overlaps the lower border of the postcard, but you'll take care of this issue in a minute

3. Click an insertion point at the right end of the e-mail address, and press **Enter** to add a new line.

    Don't worry if the Text in Overflow indicator appears again; you'll fix that next.

4. To quickly adjust the text size to make room for the web address on the new line you just added, click anywhere in the text, press **Ctrl+A** to select all the text in the text box's story, click the arrow to the right of the **Font Size** box to display a drop-down list of sizes, and click **6**.

    Publisher adjusts the font size to make room in the text box for the new line.

5. Press **End** to move to the end of the selection, type *Web: www.adworks.tld*, and then resize the box again if you need to do so.

    Now you need to move the text box so that it fits inside the business card's parameters.

6. Right-click the text box, click **Format Text Box** on the shortcut menu, and when the Format Text Box dialog box appears, click the **Layout** tab.

    The Layout tab displays the options shown in this graphic:

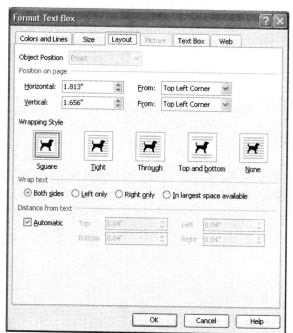

You need to instruct Publisher not to automatically adjust the text when you move its text box.

7. In the **Wrapping Style** area, click **Tight**, and then click **OK**.

8. Next point to the red dots that separate the address text box from the phone, fax, and electronic contact information text box, and when the pointer changes to a four-headed arrow, click the dots to select them.

The selection appears as shown in this graphic:

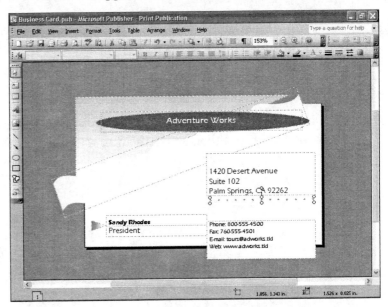

9. Hold down the **Shift** key, click the address text box, and still holding down the **Shift** key, click the contact information text box.

All three elements on the business card are now selected.

10. Click the **Group Objects** button at the bottom of the contact information text box to turn the three elements into a single unit.

11. Point to the top of the group's text box (the top of the address text box), and when the pointer changes to a four-headed arrow, drag the grouped unit upward until it just touches the bottom of the **Adventure Works** oval.

12. Click anywhere away from the group to survey your work, and then save the business card (printing it if you want to).

The business card now looks like the one shown in this graphic:

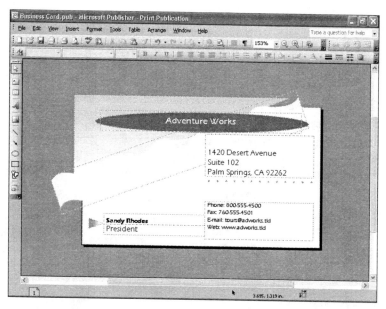

13. Close the business card by clicking **Close** on the **File** menu.

GETTING HELP

This tour of Publisher has covered a lot of ground, and you might be wondering how you will manage to retain it all. Don't worry. If you forget how to carry out a particular task, help is never far away.

You've already seen how the ScreenTips feature can jog your memory about the functions of the toolbar buttons and help you figure out the parts of a publication. And you might have noticed that the dialog boxes contain a Help button (the ? in the upper-right corner), which you can click to get information about their options. You might have also seen some tippages appear with brief pointers. Now we'll show you how to search for help using some of Publisher's other Help features.

INFORMATION ABOUT
Tippages, page 19

USING THE RESEARCH SERVICE

If you need to look up supporting information for your publication, you might want to use the Research service. By displaying the Research task pane, you can search on topics using a variety of reference sources, such as Encarta or eLibrary. The resources available from the task pane also include a thesaurus, for when you're searching for just the right word. You can even copy and paste a selection right into your document.

SEARCHING FOR HELP

First, you'll look at some ways to get information using the "Type a question for help" box at the right end of the menu bar. Follow these steps:

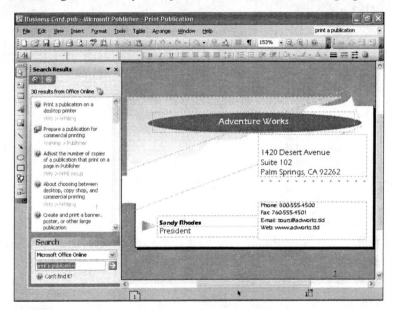

1. Click an insertion point in the **Type a question for help** box at the right end of the menu bar, type *Print a publication*, and press **Enter**.

    The Search Results task pane appears with a list of topics that might answer your question, as shown in this graphic:

2. Click the **Print a publication on a desktop printer** link.

WHAT HAPPENED TO THE OFFICE ASSISTANT?

Many Office 2003 products no longer display the Office Assistant automatically, but it is still available if you want to use it. On the Help menu, click Show the Office Assistant. The Office Assistant remains on the screen until you hide it by either right-clicking it and clicking Hide, or by clicking Hide the Office Assistant on the Help menu. (The default installation of Publisher 2003 does not include the Office Assistant. If you decide you want to use this feature, click Show the Office Assistant, and follow the prompts to install it from your Office 2003 installation CD.)

As in earlier versions of Office programs, if the Office Assistant displays a light bulb above its icon, you can click the light bulb to see a tip. To move the Office Assistant to another place on the screen, drag it. If having the Office Assistant on the screen bothers you or if you would like to customize it, you can click the Office Assistant's Options button to open the Office Assistant dialog box. Here you can select and deselect various options that control such Office Assistant characteristics as when it appears, whether it makes sounds, and which tips it displays. To turn off the Office Assistant permanently after you have initially displayed it, deselect the Use the Office Assistant check box. On the Gallery tab, you can click the Back or Next buttons to scroll through the animated characters available for the assistant (the default is Clippit, the animated paper clip) and then click OK to change the assistant. (You might need to insert the installation CD-ROM to finish the switch.)

Publisher displays the Microsoft Office Publisher Help window shown in this graphic:

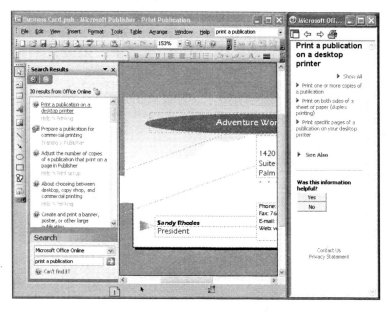

3. Read the information, and then click **Print specific pages of a publication on your desktop printer** to display instructions for that task.

4. Click the other two options to explore their tasks.

QUITTING PUBLISHER

You have seen how to use Publisher to create three simple text-based publications. Easy, wasn't it? All that's left is to show you how to end a Publisher session. Let's use a menu command to quit Publisher, like this:

1. On the **File** menu, click **Exit**.

2. If a message box appears asking whether you want to save the changes you have made to the current publication, click **Yes**.

Here are some other ways to quit Publisher:

- Click the **Close** button at the right end of Publisher's title bar.

- Press **Alt**, and then press **F** (the underlined letter in File on the menu bar), and then press **X** (the underlined letter in Exit on the File menu).

- Double-click the **Control menu** icon (the P with the sheet of paper) at the left end of Publisher's title bar.

OTHER WAYS TO GET HELP

To access the Help window without using the "Type a question for help" box, click Microsoft Office Publisher Help on the Help menu, click the Microsoft Office Publisher Help button on the Standard toolbar, or press the F1 key. The Table of Contents link in the Publisher Help task pane displays various topics represented by book icons and their subtopics represented by question mark icons. To display a topic's subtopics, click the book icon. When you find the subtopic you're looking for, click it to display the information in the Microsoft Office Publisher Help window. To access the Answer Wizard, display the Publisher Help task pane, type a question in the "Search for" box, and then click the "Start searching" button. When Help displays a list of topics that most closely fit your question, you can double-click one of the topics to display its contents in the right pane of the Help window. If you have a modem and are connected to the Internet, you can access the Microsoft Office Online web site to get information or technical support. On the Help menu, click Microsoft Office Online to display the site's home page.

DEVELOPING MORE COMPLEX PUBLICATIONS

In Chapter 1, you created two simple publications with very little fuss by using Publisher's preset designs. But as useful as these designs are, they don't always produce exactly the look you want, and you will often want to customize your publication to produce the right effect. In this chapter, you first use several task panes to create a flyer for Adventure Works, and then you customize the flyer to change how it looks.

When you have finished with this chapter, you will know how to:

- Create publications by using design sets
- Reuse information from other publications
- Work with text boxes
- Format words and paragraphs
- Work with bulleted lists
- Format with styles

Add a fancy touch
with a dropped
capital letter.

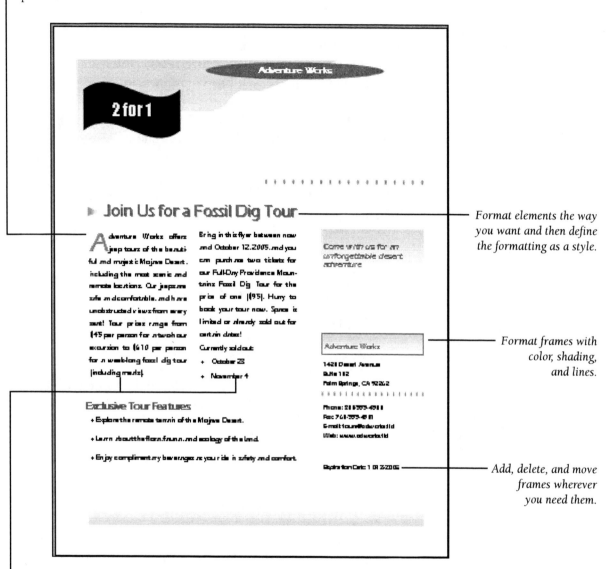

Format elements the way
you want and then define
the formatting as a style.

Format frames with
color, shading,
and lines.

Add, delete, and move
frames wherever
you need them.

Set up a multi-column
format to create a
"newspaper" look.

CREATING PUBLICATIONS BY USING DESIGN SETS

Most businesses and organizations use a common design and color scheme for all their promotional materials so that when people see a promotional piece, they immediately identify it with the business or organization. To make this practice easier, Publisher provides several design sets, which allow you to quickly create different types of publications with a unified design. You've already created publications using the Waves design; now you'll create and customize another publication from the Waves design set, and then update your personal information set for the new publication.

CREATING A FLYER BASED ON A MASTER SETS DESIGN

Suppose Adventure Works has decided to use the Waves design for all its publications. You want to create a special promotional flyer to match the informational postcard and business card you already created. Follow these steps:

1. Start **Publisher** by displaying the **Start** menu and clicking **All Programs**, **Microsoft Office**, and then **Microsoft Office Publisher 2003**.

   If the Microsoft Office Publisher 2003 command appears directly on the Start menu above All Programs, you can click it there, too.

SPECIAL DESIGN SETS

In addition to the design sets in the Master Sets list, you can access several specialized design sets via the New Publication task pane's Design Sets list. Personal Stationery Sets has eight templates designed for personal correspondence, including address labels, letterheads, business cards, and matching envelopes. The Special Event Sets and Fund-raiser Sets options each offer three sets of templates geared toward special events or fund-raisers. Holiday Sets includes three templates appropriate for winter holiday occasions. We've Moved Sets has four sets of templates used for change of address announcements or housewarming invitations. Restaurant Sets provides two sets of templates used for menus and restaurant web sites. Finally, Special Paper offers nine sets of templates available through a company called PaperDirect, which produces colored and patterned paper. If you use one of these design templates for a publication, Publisher shows you what the publication will look like when printed on PaperDirect's specialty paper.

2. In the **New Publication** task pane on the left side of the screen, click **Design Sets**, and then click **Master Sets** in the drop-down list.

   If the New Publication task pane is not displayed, you can display it by clicking the Task Pane command on the View menu, and then clicking New Publication on the task pane title bar's menu. In addition to offering design options for different print publications, web sites, and e-mail, the New Publication task pane also lists 45 basic design sets available in Publisher's Master Sets list, which is displayed in the Master Sets pane in the work area, as shown in this graphic:

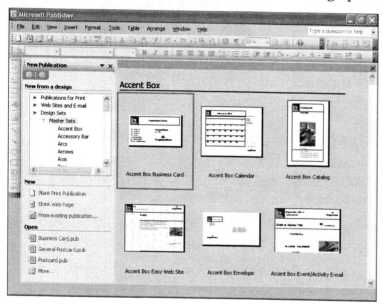

3. In the **New Publication** task pane, scroll to the end of the **Master Sets** list, click **Waves**, and then scroll through the Waves pane in the work area.

   Notice that Publisher displays all the thumbnails for publications that use the Waves design template.

4. Click the **Waves Special Offer Flyer** thumbnail.

   Publisher displays the Flyer Options task pane and opens a new special offer flyer in the right pane.

5. If Publisher displays a message box telling you it needs to install a graphics filter, click **Yes**.

INSTALL ON DEMAND

If you try to use a Publisher component or feature that is not installed, Publisher displays a message. To install the missing item, click Yes in the message box. Publisher might prompt you to insert the installation CD-ROM. When the installation is complete, Publisher loads the component or feature. This install on demand capability allows you to install items as you need them rather than storing items on your hard drive that you might never need to use.

Your screen now appears as shown in this graphic:

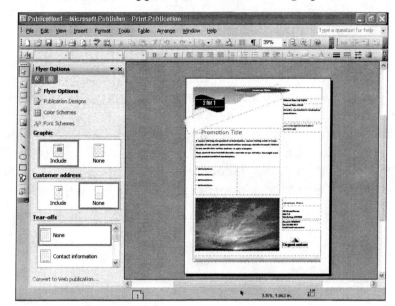

SELECTING LAYOUT AND COLOR OPTIONS

You can use the layout and color scheme provided by a design set, or you can tailor them to your own needs. Let's select layout and color options for the new flyer:

1. In the **Graphic** area of the **Flyer Options** task pane, click **None** to remove the graphic placeholder.

2. Make sure **None** is also selected in both the **Customer address** and **Tear-offs** areas of the task pane.

3. Now click the **Color Schemes** link at the top of the task pane to display the **Color Schemes** task pane, and then click **Tropics** in the **Apply a color scheme** list.

4. Click the task pane's **Close** button to expand the space available for the new flyer in Publisher's window.

    The results are shown in this graphic (we've scrolled the publication a bit to center it):

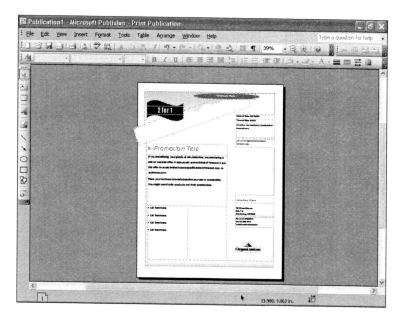

5. Click **Save As** on the **File** menu, and save the file as *Flyer* in the My Documents folder.

REUSING INFORMATION FROM OTHER PUBLICATIONS

Sometimes you might be able to reuse information from an existing publication. Publisher has already used the personal information you entered earlier to fill in some of the new flyer's placeholders. You can also copy and paste text from existing publications. As you'll discover, these features save you time and energy—you can copy text that you've already saved in an earlier publication into a new one so that you don't have to type the text from scratch.

ADJUSTING THE PERSONAL INFORMATION SET

You want to change some of the personal information that Publisher automatically inserts in your publications. To do this, you need to make some adjustments to the personal information set. Follow these steps:

1. Click **Personal Information** on the **Edit** menu to display the Personal Information dialog box.

2. In the **Phone, fax, and e-mail** box, click an insertion point at the end of the last line of text, press **Enter**, and then type *Web: www.adworks.tld*.

3. If necessary, add a hyphen to the word **Email** in the preceding line.

4. In the **Tag line or motto** box, double-click the word **An**, and type *Come with us for an* to replace the selected text.

5. Finally, click **Tropics** in the **Select a color scheme** drop-down list to change the color scheme for print publications to Tropics, and then click **Update**.

6. Save the flyer.

COPYING AND PASTING BETWEEN PUBLICATIONS

Suppose you want to use the text from the postcard as the basis for the text in the flyer. Follow these steps to set up the flyer and then copy and paste text between the two publications:

INFORMATION ABOUT
Zooming, page 17

1. Change the zoom percentage to 100%, and then if necessary, scroll to the section of the page that displays the *Promotion Title* placeholder.

2. Click the placeholder, press **Ctrl+A** if necessary to select its text, and type *Join Us for a Fossil Dig Tour*.

    Publisher automatically adjusts the size of the text to fit the text box.

3. Now click inside the text placeholder below the new title (beginning with *If you are offering your goods at reduced prices*), press **Ctrl+A** if necessary to select all the text in the text box, and press **Delete** to remove the text.

4. Save your changes, and then open the **Postcard** publication by clicking its name at the bottom of the **File** menu.

5. Select all the text beginning with *Adventure Works offers* by clicking in its text box and pressing **Ctrl+A**. Then click the **Copy** button on the Standard toolbar, and close the Postcard publication.

6. Back in the flyer, click an insertion point in the empty text box below the title.

7. Click the **Paste** button on the Standard toolbar to paste the text from the postcard into the text box.

8. Edit the text so that it looks like the paragraphs shown in this graphic:

We have indicated in bold the additions you should type. You should not include the bold formatting in your text.

9. If the new text doesn't fit entirely within the text box, click **AutoFit Text** on the **Format** menu, and then click **Best Fit**.

WORKING WITH TEXT BOXES

You've entered the main text of the flyer, and Publisher has entered information about your company using the Primary Business personal information set. You now want to customize the flyer, but first you need to learn more about how to work with text boxes. You learned briefly about moving and resizing text boxes already; in this chapter, we'll go into a little more detail by showing you how to size, add, delete, and move text boxes.

SIZING TEXT BOXES

Suppose you want to increase the legibility of the text in a few of the text boxes by increasing the font size. Making the text larger means the text boxes will no longer be big enough to display all the text, so you need to resize the text boxes. By using

COPYFITTING TEXT

If you enter more text in a text box than will fit, the text is stored in a place called the *overflow area,* and selecting the text box displays the Text in Overflow indicator. You can make the text fit its text box in several ways. You can decrease the font size, either by manually changing it a little at a time until everything fits or by clicking AutoFit Text and then Shrink Text On Overflow on the Format menu. Publisher reduces the size of the text until no text flows into the overflow area. If you resize the text box and want to make the text fit the new size, you can click AutoFit Text and then Best Fit on the Format menu. You can also click AutoFit Text to turn on automatic copyfitting so that Publisher will make adjustments every time you edit the text. (To turn off automatic copyfitting, click AutoFit Text and then click None.)

the rulers, you can size the text boxes to an exact setting. Follow these steps to increase the font size in a few of the text boxes and then increase the size of the text boxes:

1. Turn on the rulers by clicking **Rulers** on the **View** menu.

2. Select the tag line (the text that starts *Come with us*), click the **Font Size** down arrow on the Standard toolbar, and then click **12** in the drop-down list.

    Because you have increased the size of the text, it will no longer fit in its text box. Publisher moves the text that will not fit into the overflow area and displays the Text in Overflow indicator.

3. Point to the lower-middle handle of the text box.

    The pointer changes to a double-headed arrow showing the directions in which you can resize the text box. On the rulers at the top and left sides of the window's work area, guides indicate the pointer's position on the page.

4. To enlarge the text box, hold down the left mouse button and drag the lower-middle handle downward until the pointer guide sits at the 4-inch mark on the vertical ruler.

The text box now appears like the one shown in this graphic:

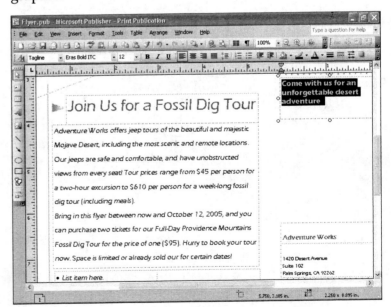

SPECIAL MOUSE POINTERS

Publisher displays special mouse pointers when you move the pointer over certain elements of a publication. To turn this feature on, click Options on the Tools menu, select the "Use helpful mouse pointers" check box on the User Assistance tab, and click OK. Then, after you select a text box, the pointer appears as a moving van with the word MOVE when it is over the text box's border, and as a double-headed arrow with the word RESIZE when it is over a handle. These pointers can be a little too cute for the experienced user, but while you are learning to use Publisher, you might want to turn them on. Otherwise, it is easy to find yourself moving a text box when you want to resize it, and vice versa. You can always turn this feature off again later when you have had more practice.

5. Click the address text box, press **Ctrl+A** to select all the text, and change the font size to **10**.

6. Next select the phone/fax/e-mail text box, select all its text, and increase the font size to **10**.

7. Point to the lower-middle handle of the phone/fax/e-mail text box, and drag to the 8.5-inch mark on the vertical ruler.

   The text (including the web address you added to the personal information set) now fits in the text box.

INFORMATION ABOUT
Personal information sets, page 7

8. Save your work.

   From now on, we won't remind you to save, so be sure to click the Save button often to safeguard your work.

ADDING AND DELETING TEXT BOXES

You want to add a subheading before the bulleted list at the bottom of the page. All text must be contained in a text box, so you need to add a text box to the flyer. You also want to get rid of some of the text boxes that Publisher includes as part of the design. Follow these steps to add the new text box and delete the old ones:

1. Scroll to bring the bulleted-list text box at the bottom of the page into view.

   The text box is currently empty, waiting for you to enter text.

2. Select the bulleted-list text box, point to the upper-middle handle, and drag the handle downward until the top of the text box is at the 8-inch mark on the vertical ruler.

3. Click the **Text Box** button on the Objects toolbar, and move the pointer over the work area.

   The pointer changes to a cross hair, waiting for you to draw a text box.

4. Point to the blue boundary line on the left side of the page, adjusting the pointer's position until the pointer guide on the vertical ruler sits at the 7.5-inch mark.

5. Hold down the left mouse button, and drag downward and to the right to draw a new text box about .5 inch tall and the same width as the bulleted-list text box below it.

MORE ABOUT SIZING
Dragging a text box's corner handles simultaneously sizes both the height and width of the text box. To size both dimensions proportionally, hold down the Shift key as you drag. When the text box reaches the size you want, release the mouse button and then the Shift key. (This procedure works for graphic frames as well as for text boxes.)

Publisher inserts the text box as shown in this graphic:

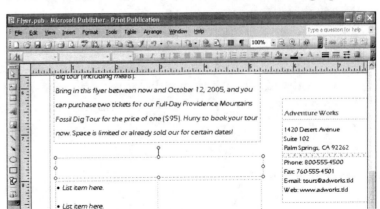

6. Type *Exclusive Tour Features* in the new text box.

   By default, the font of the text you enter in a new text box is Times New Roman, its size is 10 points, and it is aligned horizontally on the left and vertically at the top of the text box, with no other formatting.

7. Click the word **Organization** below the phone/fax/e-mail text box to select the *Logo Text* placeholder, right-click the selection, and click **Delete Object** on the shortcut menu.

8. Scroll to the top of the page, and delete the time-of-sale and the location-description text boxes.

MOVING TEXT BOXES

Now the flyer includes only the text boxes you want, but some of the text boxes would look better in different locations on the page. You already know how to move text boxes by "eyeballing" their destinations. Follow these steps to use the rulers, the Format Text Box dialog box, and ruler guides to position some of the text boxes more precisely:

1. With the top of the page still displayed, select all the text in the date-of-sale text box, and type *Expiration Date: 10-12-2005*.

2. Point to the text box's top border (not to one of its handles), hold down the left mouse button, and drag toward the bottom of the window. When you reach the bottom, continue dragging so that Publisher scrolls the hidden part of the page upward into view.

ADDING TEXT BOXES QUICKLY

You can add a text box to a page with a couple of mouse clicks. First click the Text Box button on the Objects toolbar, and then click the page. Publisher instantly draws a text box, which you can resize and reposition as necessary. You can use this same technique to quickly add any of the other drawing objects you can create with the buttons on the Objects toolbar. The exceptions are multi-layered objects such as clip art and tables, as well as "hot spot" hyperlinks and Design Gallery additions. When you click one of these buttons and then click a point on your publication, a dialog box appears so that you can provide additional information about the object you want to create.

As long as you hold down the mouse button, guides on the vertical ruler indicate the position of the top and bottom of the text box, and guides on the horizontal ruler indicate the position of the left and right sides.

3. Release the mouse button when the top of the text box sits at the 9-inch mark on the vertical ruler and the left and right sides of the text box align with the text box above it.

    The result is shown in this graphic:

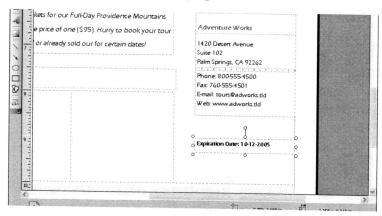

4. Now select the phone/fax/e-mail text box, click **Text Box** on the **Format** menu, and when the Format Text Box dialog box appears, click the **Layout** tab.

    Publisher displays the options shown in this graphic:

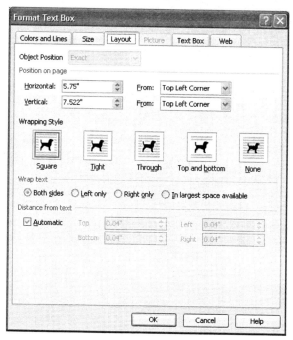

5. In the **Position on page** area at the top of the dialog box, click the **Vertical** up arrow until the setting is 7.722", and click **OK**.

Publisher adjusts the text box's position on the page. At 100%, this part of the flyer now appears as shown in this graphic:

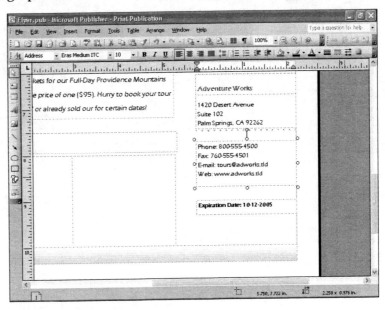

6. Scroll up until the tag-line text box comes into view.

7. Point to the horizontal ruler, and when the pointer changes to a double-headed arrow (separated in the middle by horizontal lines), drag downward until the green line attached to the pointer aligns with the bottom of the text box that contains the flyer's title (*Join Us for a Fossil Dig Tour*).

You can now use this green ruler guide to help align the top of the tag-line box with the bottom of the title text box.

8. Move the tag-line box downward until the top of the text box aligns with the green line, being careful to keep the right side of the text box aligned with the blue layout boundary line.

9. To remove the ruler guide, point to it, and drag upward to the horizontal ruler.

When you release the left mouse button, the green ruler guide disappears.

SIZING OBJECT TEXT BOXES

The default flyer design includes two text boxes that contain a row of dots: one between the address text and the phone number text, and one above the tag line. You want to change both text boxes to make them more legible and attractive. Follow these steps to reposition the text boxes on the page and change their sizes:

1. Click the dots text box above the tag-line text box, right-click the selected text box, and click **Format Object**.

2. When the Format Object dialog box appears, click the **Size** tab.

   The available options are shown in this graphic:

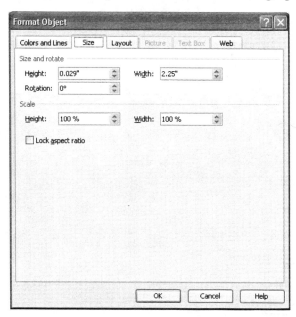

3. In the **Size and rotate** area, enter *0.1"* as the **Height** setting and *3.5"* as the **Width** setting.

RULER GUIDES VS. LAYOUT GUIDES

Ruler guides are displayed in green and appear only on the page on which you create them. Layout guides appear by default on each page of a publication. These blue lines consist of margin guides that appear at the top, bottom, left, and right sides of each page to indicate the publication's margins, and grid guides that divide the page into equal segments. You use these layout guides to position text boxes consistently from page to page and from publication to publication. To adjust them, click Layout Guides on the Arrange menu. You can then change the position of the margin guides and display more or fewer grid guides. To hide all the guides so that you get a better idea of how a page will look when printed, click Boundaries and Guides on the View menu to remove the check mark and toggle this command off. To redisplay all the guides, click Boundaries and Guides again.

4. Click the **Layout** tab, and enter *4.5"* as the **Horizontal** setting and *2.94"* as the **Vertical** setting. Then click OK.

5. Now scroll to the dots text box between the address text and phone number text, click the text box to select it, and click **Object** on the **Format** menu.

   If you have trouble selecting the dots text box, increase the zoom percentage, and then click one of the dots.

6. Click the **Size** tab, and in the **Size and rotate** area, enter *0.1"* as the **Height** setting.

7. Click the **Layout** tab, and in the **Position on page** area, enter *7.57"* as the **Vertical** setting. Then click OK.

8. Click **Rulers** on the **View** menu to turn off the rulers.

9. Finally, change the zoom setting to **50%**, and click a blank part of the work area so that you can see the main features of the flyer.

   The flyer now looks similar to the one shown in this graphic:

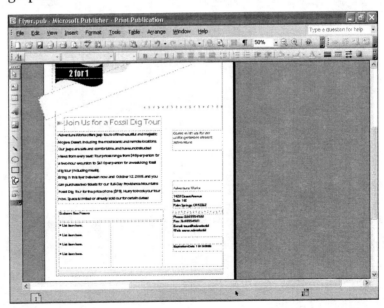

FORMATTING WORDS AND PARAGRAPHS

When you use one of Publisher's design sets to create a publication, the program makes a lot of decisions for you about how various elements will look. However, as you just saw, when you add a new text element to a publication, Publisher applies very little formatting, under the assumption that you will want to control the appearance of the new element yourself. In this topic, you learn a variety of methods for changing the look of words and paragraphs.

FORMATTING TEXT

Headings are the most important elements in promotional publications. Their job is to grab the attention of your readers, draw them in, and make them want to read further. So headings should always be formatted in such a way that they catch the readers' eye.

The new heading that you just added to the flyer looks plain and unremarkable. As it is, the heading would likely go unnoticed. Follow these steps to make the headings in the flyer stand out:

1. Press **F9** to zoom to 100%, select the text of the **Exclusive Tour Features** heading, and then click the **Font** box down arrow on the Formatting toolbar to display a list of the available fonts.

    Times New Roman ▾

2. Scroll the list upward, and then click **Eras Medium ITC** to change the font to match the rest of the flyer.

3. Click the **Font Size** down arrow on the Formatting toolbar, and then click **16**.

4. Next click the **Bold** button on the Formatting toolbar to make the selected text bold.

    B

5. With the text still selected, right-click it, and then click **Format Text Box** on the shortcut menu. When the Format Text Box dialog box appears, click the **Text Box** tab.

COPYING FORMATS

If you want to apply all of the formatting from a block of text or text box to another block or text box, you can use the Format Painter to copy all the formatting in a simple three-step procedure. Select the text with the formatting you want to copy, click the Format Painter button on the Standard toolbar, and then select the text you want to format. Publisher duplicates the formatting for the new selection.

The options on the Text Box tab appear as shown in this graphic:

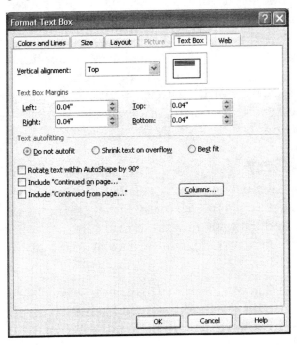

6. In the **Vertical alignment** drop-down list, click **Bottom**, and then click **OK**.

The results are shown in this graphic:

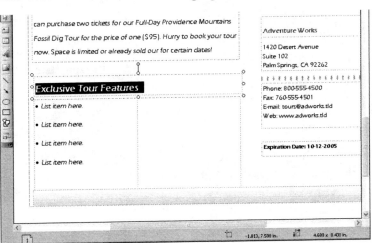

TRUE TYPE FONTS

When you print most fonts on paper, they appear the same way they do on the screen because most printer fonts have a corresponding screen font. For those that don't, Publisher chooses the closest match, which can cause layout problems because of differences in character spacing or letter size. Publisher recommends that you use only TrueType fonts, which have both screen and printer components, so that what you see on-screen is what you get on paper. TrueType fonts are identified by a TT symbol to the left of the font name in the font list.

7. If necessary, scroll upward, select the words **Adventure Works** in the oval at the top of the page, change the size of the selection to **14**, and then make it bold.

8. Select the flyer's title, and click **Font** on the **Format** menu.

Publisher displays this dialog box:

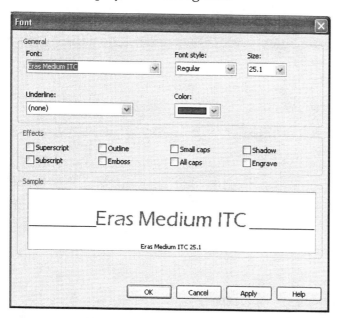

The settings in the dialog box reflect the character formatting of the selected title. As you can see, the dialog box provides several options not available on the Formatting toolbar.

9. Click **Bold** in the **Font style** list, select the **Shadow** check box in the **Effects** area, and then click **OK**.

If you want, you can experiment with some of the other options in the Font dialog box before moving on.

CHARACTER SPACING

In the publishing world, the adjustment of spacing between characters is called kerning. Tighter kerning pulls characters together, and looser kerning pushes them apart. Awkward character spacing is more evident with large text, such as in headlines, so by default, Publisher adjusts the kerning between certain character pairs when the point size is greater than 14. You can change Publisher's kerning setting or turn it off by clicking Character Spacing on the Format menu. In the "Automatic pair kerning" area, adjust the point size at which kerning kicks in or deselect the "Kern text at" check box to turn off automatic kerning altogether. To manually kern a character pair, first select the characters, and then click Character Spacing on the Format menu. In the Kerning area, click the arrow to the right of the text box, and click Expand to increase the amount of space between the characters or Condense to decrease the amount of space. Then enter an amount in the "By this amount" box. To adjust the spacing of a large block of text, use the Tracking area of the Character Spacing dialog box. To adjust the width of selected characters rather than the spacing between them, use the Scaling area.

ADDING BORDERS

INFORMATION ABOUT
BorderArt, page 102

To emphasize a particular text box, you can add borders above and below or to the left and right of it, or you can surround certain paragraphs within the text box with borders of various styles. Place a border around the organization name by following these steps:

1. Select the organization name text box above the address text box (not the one in the oval at the top of the flyer).

2. Click the **Line/Border Style** button on the Formatting toolbar.

   Publisher displays the palette shown in this graphic.

3. Click the thickest of the solid line-style options.

   The text box now looks like the one shown in this graphic:

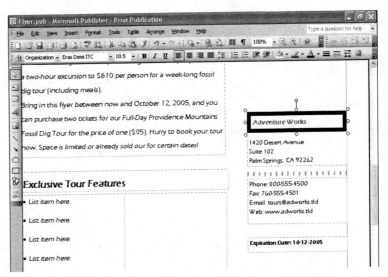

4. You don't like this effect, so click the **Undo** button.

DRAWING LINES

Instead of the thick black border you applied (and then undid) in the last procedure, suppose you want to draw a line across the bottom of the text box to visually separate the company name from the address. Then you want to add some shading to the text box. Follow these steps to add this formatting:

1. With the organization name text box above the address text box still selected, click the **Line/Border Style** button again, and then click **More Lines** in the drop-down palette.

    Publisher displays the Colors and Lines tab of the Format Text Box dialog box, as shown in this graphic:

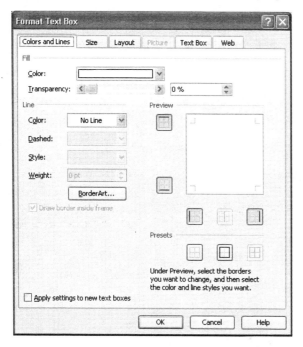

2. In the **Line** area, click the **Color** down arrow, and click the slate-blue color box (**Accent 1**, or the second box in the colors row).

    The color of the line now matches the color of the text of the Adventure Works organization name.

3. Leave the **Dashed** and **Style** settings as they are, and then click the **Weight** up arrow until the setting is **2 pt**.

4. Click **OK** when you have finished, and save your work.

ADDING PAGE BORDERS

You can put a border around each page of a publication by clicking the Rectangle button on the Objects toolbar and drawing a rectangle around all the objects on the page. When you release the mouse button, Publisher adds a black, 0.75-point border. To change the line thickness or color, click the Line/Border Style button and then click More Lines. Select the options you want and click OK. To repeat a border on every page, you can copy and paste the first border to all subsequent pages. To add border graphics rather than lines, you can use BorderArt.

ADDING SHADING

Now let's add some shading to the text box to make it stand out even more. Follow these steps:

1. With the organization name text box still selected, click the **Fill Color** down arrow on the Formatting toolbar.

    Publisher displays the palette shown in this graphic:

    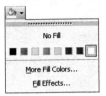

2. Click the gold color box (**Accent 2**, or the third box in the colors row) to apply that color to the selected text box.

3. Click the **Fill Color** down arrow again, and then click **Fill Effects**.

    The Fill Effects dialog box appears, as shown in this graphic:

    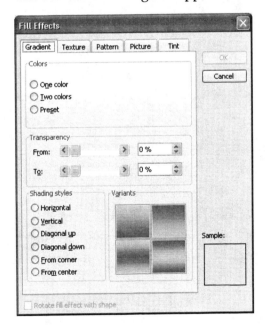

In this dialog box, you can change the tint or shade of the selected color and apply a pattern or gradient to the shading.

4. With the **Gradient** tab displayed, click the first gradient in the first row of the **Variants** area.

   Now the preset gradient is too dark for the text inside the text box to be legible.

5. Slide the **Dark/Light** slider control in the **Colors** area all the way to **Light**, and then click **OK** to implement the changes.

6. Repeat steps 1 through 5 to apply the same shading color, gradient pattern, and lightness to the tag-line text box.

7. With the tag-line text box still selected, click **Text Box** on the **Format** menu, and when the Format Text Box dialog box appears, click the **Text Box** tab.

8. Click the **Vertical alignment** down arrow, click **Bottom**, and then click **OK** to apply the alignment change.

   The results are shown in this graphic:

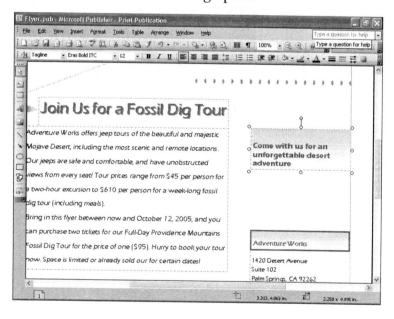

CHANGING TEXT COLOR

When you add a border or shading, the formatting affects the entire text box. However, when you change the text color, the change affects only the selected text. Let's change the color of the heading you added earlier:

1. Scroll the *Exclusive Tour Features* heading into view.

USING NON-COLOR-SCHEME COLORS

To use a color that is not part of the color scheme defined by the design set, click More Colors on the Font Color button's palette to display the Colors dialog box. You can then either click a color on the Standard tab or define a color by clicking the Custom tab, clicking an area in the color palette, and then moving the slider on the luminescence scale. However, if you use a color that is not part of the color scheme, your selection might not coordinate with the other colors in the publication. If you later decide to change the color scheme, the color you selected remains applied, whereas Publisher adjusts the other colors to reflect the new color scheme.

2. Select the heading text, and click the **Font Color** down arrow on the Formatting toolbar.

    Publisher displays a palette, which you can use to apply color to the selected text in much the same way you apply it to a text box. You can select one of the current scheme's colors or select a color from a different scheme. You can also select a custom color and add fill effects.

3. If you want, experiment with some of the colors, and then finish by clicking the slate-blue color box (**Accent 1**, or the second box in the colors row).

    The color of the heading now matches that of other headings in the flyer.

ADDING A DROP CAP

A simple way to add a designer touch to a publication is to use Publisher's built-in drop cap (for *dropped capital letter*) format. You might want to enhance newsletters, reports, and other publications intended for public viewing by adding drop caps. As a demonstration, let's insert a drop cap in the first paragraph of the flyer's main text:

1. Scroll to the paragraph below the flyer's title, and click an insertion point to the left of the first line (the one that begins with *Adventure Works offers*).

2. Click **Drop Cap** on the **Format** menu.

    The Drop Cap dialog box appears, as shown in this graphic:

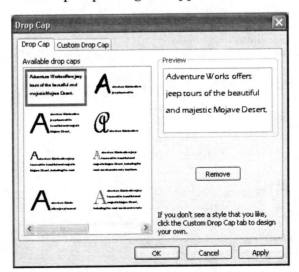

Publisher displays several drop cap styles in the "Available drop caps" area. You can select any style and view its results in the Preview box on the right. If none of the styles fits your needs, you can create your own drop cap style.

3. Scroll the **Available drop caps** area to see what's available.

None of the preset drop cap designs seems to fit your flyer, but you can use Publisher's custom drop cap feature to create a drop cap that is appropriate for the Flyer publication's theme.

4. Click the **Custom Drop Cap** tab.

Publisher displays the options shown in this graphic:

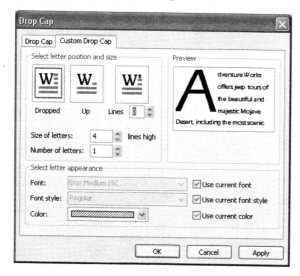

5. With the **Dropped** option selected, change the **Size of letters** setting to 2.

6. Deselect both the **Use current font style** and **Use current color** check boxes, but leave the **Use current font** check box selected.

7. Change the **Font style** setting to **Bold** and the **Color** setting to the red color box (**Accent 3**, or the fourth box in the colors row).

8. Click **OK** to close the dialog box and apply the new drop cap to the letter *A* in *Adventure Works*.

9. Select the drop cap, and click **Font** on the **Format** menu. Then in the **Effects** area, select the **Shadow** check box, and in the **General** area, change the font size to **8.5** by typing over the current entry.

10. Click **OK** to apply the drop cap changes.

The results are shown in this graphic:

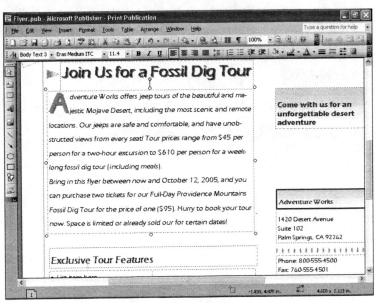

SETTING UP MULTIPLE COLUMNS

Flyers and newsletters often feature multi-column layouts like those used in magazines and newspapers. With these layouts, you have more flexibility in placing elements on the page, and multi-column layouts are frequently more visually interesting than single-column layouts. To demonstrate how easy it is to set up multiple columns in Publisher, let's change the body text of the flyer to a two-column format. Follow these steps:

1. Click the flyer's body text text box (the one containing the new drop cap) to select it. Then click the **Columns** button on the Formatting toolbar.

A palette of columns appears, as shown in this graphic:

2. Move the mouse pointer over the second column in the palette.

   Publisher highlights the first two columns and displays the words *2 Columns* at the bottom of the palette, as shown in this graphic:

3. Click the second column, and when Publisher displays a message warning you that copyfitting cannot be used on columns of text, click **Yes** to proceed.

4. Next click **Text Box** on the **Format** menu, click the **Text Box** tab, and then click **Columns**.

   The Columns dialog box appears, as shown in this graphic:

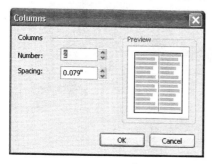

   The Columns option is not available in the Format Text Box dialog box until you convert a text box into columns using the Formatting toolbar's Columns button, as you just did.

5. Click the **Spacing** up arrow until the setting is *0.279″*, and then click **OK** twice to close both the Columns and Format Text Box dialog boxes.

   The results are shown in the graphic on the next page.

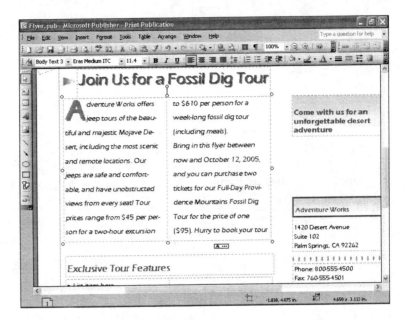

As you can see, the flyer would look better if the second paragraph of text started at the top of the second column.

6. Resize the body text text box so that its bottom border touches the top border of the *Exclusive Tour Features* text box, and change the font size to 10.5.

The columns of body text now appear similar to the ones in this graphic:

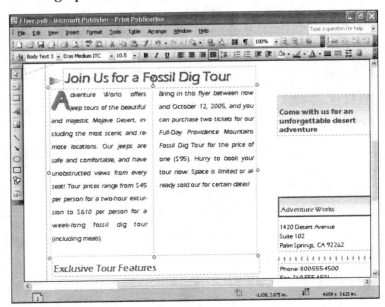

MORE TEXT BOX PROPERTIES

In addition to changing the number of columns in a parti- cular text box, you can make other adjustments in the For- mat Text Box dialog box. In the Margins area of the Text Box tab, you can adjust the amount of space between the text box and its contents. Below the "Text autofitting" area (which is disabled for text formatted as columns), you can select or deselect check boxes that deter- mine whether text in the text box rotates around AutoShapes. With these check boxes, you can also control whether a "Continued on page" or "Con- tinued from page" line appears in the text box to help readers move through a multi-text box story.

JUSTIFYING PARAGRAPHS

You have already seen how to align text vertically in its text box. You can also align text horizontally to the left, right, or center of its text box by using the corresponding buttons on the For-matting toolbar. For a professional look, however, you might want text to be aligned neatly at both edges of the text box. Called *justification*, this type of alignment adds space between the words on a line to spread them evenly across the text box. As a final touch, let's justify the flyer's body text. Try this:

1. Select the text of both paragraphs, and click the **Justify** button on the Formatting toolbar.

   Publisher justifies the paragraphs so that their lines are even with both the left and right edges of the text box. Here are the results at 66% magnification:

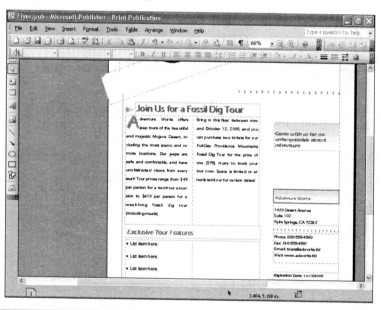

HYPHENATING PUBLICATIONS

By default, Publisher hyphenates the text in some text boxes, including those you create with the Text Box tool. To turn off hyphenation for a particular text box, select the text box, click Language and then Hyphenation on the Tools menu, deselect the "Automatically hyphenate this story" check box, and then click OK. You will want to leave hyphenation turned on if the text is justified, because it eliminates big gaps between words. For left-aligned paragraphs, you can change the hyphenation zone (the space between the right margin and the end of the text line) by entering a new measurement in the "Hyphen-ation zone" text box of the Hyphenation dialog box. If you keep the hyphenation zone small, the right side of your text will be less ragged, but more words will be hyphenated. If you increase the hyphenation zone, the raggedness will be more pronounced but fewer words will be hyphenated. To manually hy-phenate text, deselect the "Automatically hyphenate this story" check box, and click the Manual button. Publisher then displays each word that can be hyphenated. Click Yes to hyphenate the word, or click No to leave it unhyphenated.

2. To see the results of your hard work on paper, click the **Print** button on the Standard toolbar.

WORKING WITH BULLETED LISTS

Bulleted lists provide a simple way for you to display information in a concise, easy-to-read fashion. Publisher has already inserted a bulleted-list placeholder in the flyer for you; you just need to fill in the list with your own text. When you're finished with that, you'll want to format the list so that it looks just the way you want it.

FILLING IN A LIST

The text box on the left at the bottom of the flyer contains four bulleted items that are waiting for your text. Follow these steps to fill in the bulleted list:

1. Scroll to the bulleted-list text box, and then click the text box to select it.

   This text box is set up for two columns, but you want only one.

2. Double-click the border of the text box to display the Format Text Box dialog box, click the **Text Box** tab, and then click **Columns**.

3. In the Columns dialog box, change the number of columns to 1, and click **OK** twice to remove the multiple-column format.

4. Press **Ctrl+A** to select all the bulleted iems. Then type the following, pressing **Enter** after each line except the last to add a new bulleted item:

   Explore the remote terrain of the Mojave Desert.

   Learn about the flora, fauna, and ecology of the land.

   Enjoy complimentary beverages as you ride in safety and comfort.

CHANGING THE BULLET CHARACTER IN A BULLETED LIST

INFORMATION ABOUT
Inserting special symbols, page 82

The plain round bullet characters in the new bulleted list look a little boring for a flyer about travel, so let's make them a little more exciting. Follow these steps:

1. With the bulleted-list text box still selected, press **Ctrl+A** to select all the bulleted items, and then click **Bullets and Numbering** on the **Format** menu.

   Publisher displays the Bullets and Numbering dialog box, as shown in this graphic:

   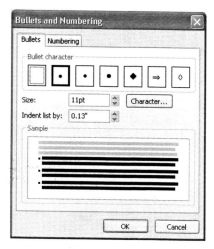

   You can choose one of the six suggested bullet shapes or click the Character button to select other options.

2. Click the diamond shape, and then click **OK**.

   The bullets change, as shown in this graphic:

   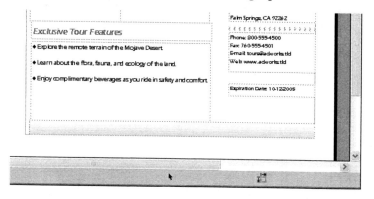

CONVERTING EXISTING TEXT TO A BULLETED LIST

You can quickly convert existing text paragraphs to a bulleted list by selecting the paragraphs and clicking the Bullets button on the Formatting toolbar. You can then use the Bullets and Numbering dialog box to customize the list. Let's get some

MORE LIST OPTIONS

In the Bullets and Numbering dialog box, you can change a bullet's size and indent settings, as well as its character. (The Bullet Character dialog box works like the Insert Symbol dialog box.) To convert a bulleted list to a numbered list, select the Numbering tab to display numbered list options, such as the number format and the separator type (the separator is the character immediately following the number—a period, for example). To convert the list to regular text, select the first, blank character in the "Bullet character" section and click OK.

practice by inserting some new text and converting it into bullets:

1. In the main body-text box, click an insertion point after the exclamation point following *dates!* at the end of the second paragraph, and press the **Enter** key to insert another line.

2. On the new line, type *Currently sold out:* (include the colon after *out*). Press **Enter** again, type *October 23*, press **Enter**, and then type *November 4*.

3. Select both the **October 23** and **November 4** paragraphs, and then click the **Bullets** button on the Formatting toolbar.

   Publisher converts the paragraphs into bulleted items, inserting the diamond character you previously set for the bullets.

FORMATTING WITH STYLES

A style is the collection of formatting applied to a particular block of text. Every paragraph you write is formatted with a style. When you create a new text box in a publication, Publisher by default applies the Normal style to any paragraphs you type. The Normal style formats text in the Times New Roman font and makes it 10 points in size, and it left aligns and single-spaces each paragraph. You can change this default formatting by applying different formats one by one, or by applying a style that includes all the formats.

As you might have noticed while working in the publications you have created, each of Publisher's design sets comes with a collection of built-in styles. When you click in a paragraph or select any of its text, the style currently applied to the paragraph or the text is displayed in the Style box on the Formatting toolbar. You can apply any available style by clicking it in the Style drop-down list.

If none of the available styles meets your needs, you can define a combination of formatting as a custom style and then apply that style in the same way. In this topic, you'll explore two ways of creating styles that you will apply to the paragraphs of the flyer.

CREATING A STYLE FROM EXISTING TEXT

Follow these steps to see how to quickly create a new style using the formatting that already exists in the flyer's text elements:

1. Select the **Join Us** title text, and click the **Style** box at the left end of the Formatting toolbar once to highlight the name of the current style.

2. Type *Flyer Title* as the new style name, and press **Enter**.

   The Create Style By Example dialog box appears, as shown in this graphic:

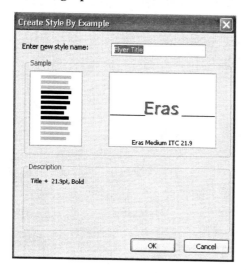

3. Verify that the new style has the correct formatting, and then click **OK**.

   Publisher creates the style, adds its name to the Style list, and displays Flyer Title in the Style box to identify the style applied to the active paragraph.

4. Click an insertion point in the **Exclusive Tour Features** heading, click the **Style** down arrow, and click **Flyer Title** in the drop-down list.

   Publisher changes the style of the heading so that its formatting is consistent with the title. After you see the effect of changing the style, you decide you don't like it.

5. Click the **Undo** button on the Standard toolbar to reinstate the previous formatting.

CREATING A STYLE FROM SCRATCH

Now turn your attention to the main text paragraphs of the flyer. Suppose you want to change the font, add a little space before each paragraph, and adjust the spacing between lines. Follow these steps to create a new style that includes all of those elements:

1. Click an insertion point in the first body text paragraph of the flyer, and click **Styles and Formatting** on the **Format** menu.

   The Styles and Formatting task pane appears, as shown here:

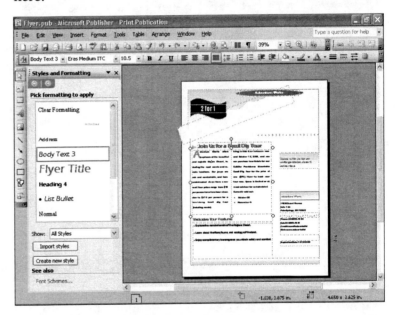

   In the Styles and Formatting task pane, you can apply an existing style; add a new style; modify, rename, or delete the selected style; or import styles from a different publication.

IMPORTING STYLES

After you create a style for use in one publication, you don't have to recreate it for use in others. Instead, you can import the style. Open the publication where you want to use the style, click the "Import styles" button in the Styles and Formatting task pane, and in the Import Styles dialog box, navigate to the appropriate publication file, and double-click it to import its styles into the current publication. To import styles from a file created in another program, click the "Files of type" down arrow in the Import Styles dialog box, select the program the file was created in, navigate to the file, and then double-click it. (If the file type is not listed, you can't import its styles into Publisher.)

2. Click the **Create new style** button at the bottom of the **Styles and Formatting** task pane.

Publisher displays the New Style dialog box shown in this graphic:

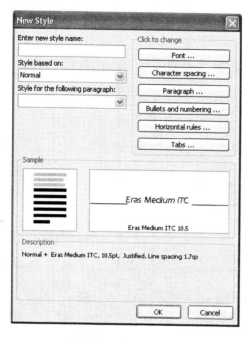

3. Type *Flyer Text* in the **Enter new style name** box, and then click the **Font** button in the **Click to change** area to display the Font dialog box.

4. Make sure the font is set to **Eras Medium ITC**, change the font size to 11, and click **OK**.

5. Next click the **Paragraph** button in the **Click to change** area, and if necessary, click the **Indents and Spacing** tab.

MODIFYING STYLES

To modify a style, first open the Styles and Formatting task pane, click the arrow to the right of the style you want to modify in the "Pick formatting to apply" area, and click Modify. Make the necessary formatting changes in the Modify Style dialog box, and then click OK to implement the changes. When you redefine a style, all occurrences of that style in your current publication are updated.

You can also make formatting changes directly to the text containing a style and then click "Update to match selection" on the affected style's drop-down menu. All the paragraphs containing this style will be updated to reflect the changes.

Publisher displays the dialog box shown in this graphic:

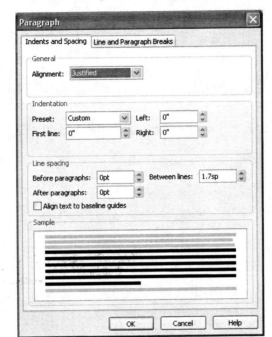

6. Change the **Between lines** setting in the **Line spacing** area by typing *1.5sp*. Then change the **Before paragraphs** setting to *3pt* and the **After paragraphs** setting to *0pt*.

7. Click **OK** twice to close both the Paragraph and the New Style dialog boxes.

APPLYING A STYLE

You apply a style to instantly format words and paragraphs, But sometimes you might want a particular paragraph to have some but not all of a style's formats. In that case, you must decide whether to apply the style and then manually change the format that isn't quite right, or whether to apply the formats individually. Follow these steps to see the difference:

1. Click an insertion point in the first paragraph, and then click **Flyer Text** in the **Pick formatting to apply** list of the **Styles and Formatting** task pane.

   Publisher applies the formatting of the new style to the paragraph.

2. Now click an insertion point in the second paragraph (but not in the sold-out bulleted list or its title). Repeat step 1 to apply the new style to the second paragraph.

Publisher applies the formatting of the new style to the second paragraph.

Now you want to make the line spacing of the *Currently sold out* text and its small bulleted list more consistent with the new Flyer Text style. Applying the new style to this bulleted list is not a good idea, because it will overwrite the list's formatting. Complete the following step instead.

3. Select the **Currently sold out** text and its two bullets, and click **Paragraph** on the **Format** menu. Type **3** in the **Before paragraph** box, press the **Tab** key, type *1.5* in the **Between lines** box, press the **Tab** key, type *0*, and then click **OK**.

4. Save your work, and if you are not continuing on to the next chapter, close Publisher.

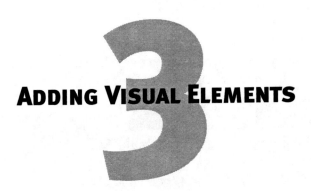

ADDING VISUAL ELEMENTS

As you followed the examples in the preceding chapters, you learned a lot about working with text and text boxes and using styles to create professional-looking publications. However, text alone is often not enough to get your point across. Most promotional materials include visual elements, both to provide information and to catch a reader's eye.

With all the clip art Publisher supplies, as well as WordArt, graphics from other applications, and Publisher's many drawing tools, you should have no trouble adding a dash of excitement to all your publications. Just remember to keep things simple; otherwise, your audience might start paying more attention to your artwork than to the message that you are ultimately trying to get across in your publication.

When you have finished with this chapter, you will know how to:

- Create a brochure
- Create a logo
- Create fancy text effects with WordArt
- Work with template tables
- Work with graphics
- Work with shapes

Draw a shape, add text, and then manipulate the object in various ways.

Add graphics from the Clip Gallery and size and position them precisely.

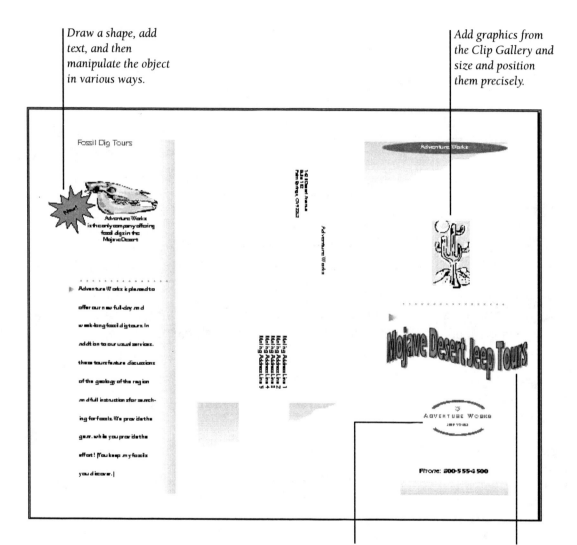

Pick an element from the Design Gallery and then customize it.

Use WordArt to create a fancy title.

CREATING A BROCHURE

In this chapter, you create a three-panel promotional brochure for Adventure Works. With a little imagination, this type of brochure can be adapted for any business, organization, club, event, or school activity.

You create a brochure the same way you create all publications in Publisher—by making selections in the New Publication task pane.

STARTING A NEW BROCHURE

Let's get started with the brochure:

1. Start **Publisher**, and in the **New Publication** task pane, click **Publications for Print** in the **New from a design** area.

2. Click **Brochures** in the **Publications for Print** list, and then click the **Price List** subcategory.

   Publisher displays thumbnails of the available price list brochure designs in the work pane.

3. In the work pane, scroll to the **Waves Price List Brochure** thumbnail, and click it.

   Publisher opens a new brochure in the work pane and displays the Brochure Options task pane.

4. Click **Include** in the **Customer address** area of the **Brochure Options** task pane.

   Publisher adds a placeholder for a customer address to the brochure.

5. Make sure that **None** is selected in the **Form** area.

6. Click the **Color Schemes** link at the top of the **Brochure Options** task pane.

   Publisher displays the Color Schemes task pane.

7. Check that **Tropics** is selected in the **Apply a color scheme** list, and then click the task pane's **Close** button.

   The brochure now appears as shown in this graphic:

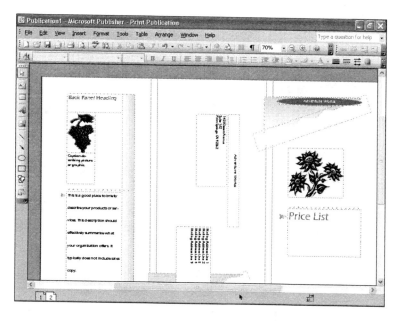

As you can see, Publisher displays the three outside panels of the brochure. To view the three inside panels, you can click the 2 button in the page navigation controls on the status bar.

8. Save the new publication in the My Documents folder as *Brochure*.

FILLING IN THE BROCHURE'S TEXT FIELDS

Before you can get started on the visual elements of the brochure, you need to add the promotional text. Follow these steps:

1. Change the zoom setting to 100%, and scroll the top of the left panel on the first page into view.

2. Select the **Back Panel Heading** placeholder at the top of the left panel, and type *Fossil Dig Tours*.

3. Scroll down, click anywhere in the text box that contains the *This is a good place* placeholder, and type the following text:

    Adventure Works is pleased to offer our new full-day and week-long fossil dig tours. In addition to our usual services, these tours feature discussions of the geology of the region and full instructions for searching for fossils. We provide the gear, while you provide the effort! (You keep any fossils you discover.)

LOREM IPSUM

In the left panel, Publisher has inserted a bunch of nonsense words as the second paragraph. This placeholder text is traditionally used in design work to give an idea of how the publication will look when real text is in place, without the distraction of words you can actually read. The origins of this tradition stem from an unknown printer who, centuries ago, took a block of text from writings by Cicero and scrambled it slightly in order to create dummy text. Interestingly, though the words are Latin, this type of placeholder is known as *greeked text*.

4. Click the 2 button in the page controls, and scroll to the top of the left panel.

5. Click the **Main Inside Heading** placeholder, and then type *More About Our Tours*.

6. Click an insertion point to the left of the *O* in *Our*, and press **Shift+Enter**.

   Publisher breaks the line so that *Our Tours* appears on the second line.

7. Click the text box below the heading, and replace its text by typing the following three paragraphs, pressing **Enter** after each one:

   Join us on one of our unique half-day or full-day Mojave Desert jeep tours. You will be accompanied by an expert guide, who will entertain you with fact-filled commentary on the flora, fauna, geology, and history of this fascinating area.

   All tours are conducted in air-conditioned luxury four-wheel-drive vehicles, each of which is fully stocked with food, beverages, and first-aid kits.

   Call today to sign up for the adventure of a lifetime!

8. Save your work.

CREATING A LOGO

As you know, Publisher provides many design templates to help you create different types of publications. But the program also has a Design Gallery of elements that you might want to use in more than one publication.

In this topic, you take a look at the Design Gallery, insert a logo for the cover of the Adventure Works brochure, and then modify it using the Logo Options task pane.

INSERTING A DESIGN GALLERY OBJECT

Logos often include a graphic or design that helps establish a visual identity. Let's insert a graphic from the Design Gallery to use as the basis for the brochure's logo:

1. Move to page 1 of the brochure, and scroll the bottom half of the right panel into view.

2. Click the **Design Gallery Object** button on the Objects toolbar.

Publisher displays the Design Gallery dialog box, shown in this graphic:

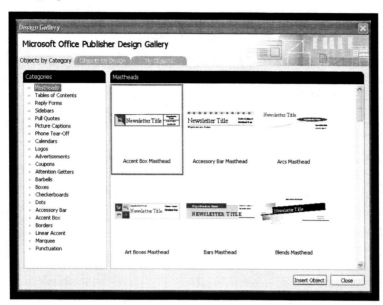

MORE ABOUT THE DESIGN GALLERY

It is worth taking the time to explore the objects available in the Design Gallery, including such useful publication elements as calendars, coupons, and attention getters like starbursts or flags. On the Objects by Design tab, you can display items grouped by design template. On the My Objects tab, you can add your own objects to the Design Gallery and then insert them in your publications. To add an object to the Design Gallery, select it in your publication, click the Design Gallery button on the Objects toolbar, and click the My Objects tab. Click the Options button in the bottom left corner and then click Add Selection to Design Gallery on the shortcut menu. In the Add Object dialog box, type a name for the object in the "Object name" text box, select a category in the Category drop-down list or type a name to create a new category, and click OK. To delete an object from the My Objects tab, click the object's thumbnail in the right pane, click the Options button, click Delete This Object, and then click OK to confirm the deletion. If you want to add, delete, or rename categories in the My Objects tab, click the Options button and then click Edit Categories. When you finish making changes in the Edit Categories dialog box, click Close.

3. In the **Categories** list in the left pane of the **Objects by Category** tab, click various headings to see the available options in the right pane.

4. Click **Logos** in the left pane, and then double-click **Open Oval Logo** in the right pane.

   Publisher inserts the object shown in this graphic on the page:

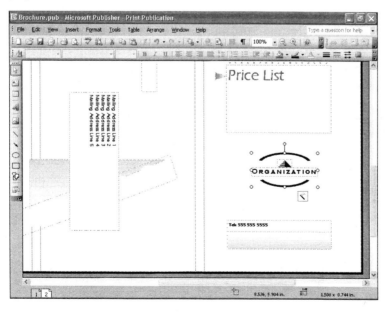

CUSTOMIZING A DESIGN GALLERY OBJECT

Now that the new logo object is inserted in your publication, you can customize it so that it looks exactly the way you want. Follow these steps:

1. Click the **Wizard** button that is attached to the new logo, and when the **Logo Designs** task pane appears, click the **Logo Options** link at the top of the task pane.

   Publisher displays the Logo Options task pane, as shown in this graphic:

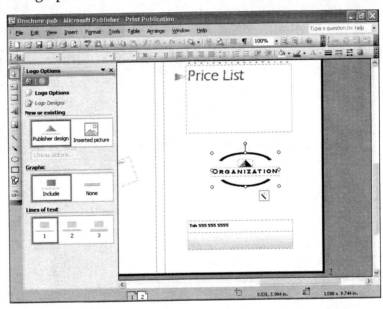

   As you can see, the Logo Options task pane provides options for using an existing picture file as a logo, inserting or removing a graphic placeholder, or changing the number of lines reserved for text. (You can also change the logo's design from the Logo Designs task pane.)

2. In the **Lines of text** area, click **2**, and then click the task pane's **Close** button.

3. Click the logo's *Organization* placeholder text box to select it, and type *Adventure Works* to replace the existing text.

   Because the placeholder text is formatted to appear as small capital letters, the words you typed appear in capital letters, even though you typed them with initial capitals only.

4. Increase the zoom setting to **200%** for better visibility. Then select the **Name** placeholder, type *Jeep Tours*, and decrease the zoom percentage to **100%** again.

5. Click the logo, and then click **Object** on the **Format** menu. On the **Layout** tab of the Format Object dialog box, type *8.5* in the **Horizontal** box, type **6** in the **Vertical** box, and click OK.

   The logo is now positioned better in relation to the telephone number text box below it, as shown in this graphic:

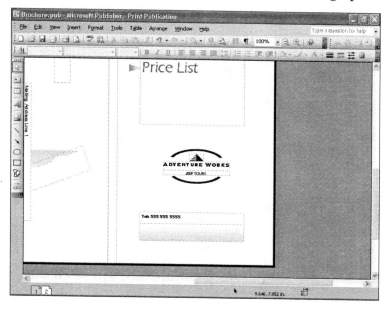

6. Select **Tel:** and the phone number in the text box below the logo, and type *Phone: 800-555-4500*.

7. To make the number more readable, click **AutoFit Text** and then **Best Fit** on the **Format** menu.

8. Finally, click the **Center** button on the Formatting toolbar to center the telephone number text in its text box.

CREATING FANCY TEXT EFFECTS WITH WORDART

You want the cover of the brochure to have a title that grabs your readers' attention, so we'll now introduce you to WordArt, a program that comes with the Office 2003 family of programs, including Publisher 2003. You can use this handy program to mold text into shapes that fit the mood of a publication.

CREATING A WORDART OBJECT

Follow the steps on the next page to jazz up the cover of the brochure with a WordArt object.

MAKING PHONE NUMBERS APPEAR AUTOMATICALLY

Publisher enters the telephone number from your personal information set only in phone/fax/e-mail text boxes. The text box containing the telephone number at the bottom of the right panel on page 1 is a plain text text box. To insert a phone/fax/e-mail text box, click Personal Information and then Phone/Fax/E-mail on the Insert menu.

1. Select the **Price List** text box in the right panel of the first page, and click **Delete Object** on the **Edit** menu to delete the text box and its text.

    You don't need this text box because you will use a WordArt frame instead.

2. Click the **Insert WordArt** button on the Objects toolbar.

    The WordArt Gallery dialog box appears, as shown in this graphic:

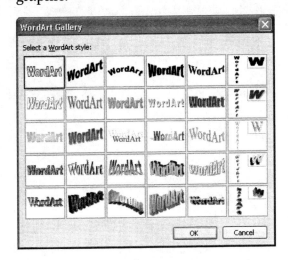

3. Click the fifth WordArt thumbnail in the fourth row (the wavy yellow one), and then click **OK**.

    The Edit WordArt Text dialog box appears, as shown in this graphic:

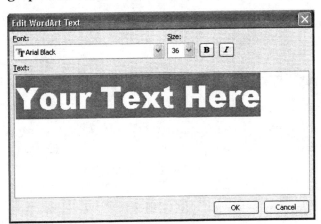

4. Replace the *Your Text Here* text in the **Text** box with *Mojave Desert Jeep Tours*. Click **Eras Bold ITC** in the **Font** drop-down list, and then click **OK**.

Publisher inserts the WordArt object into your brochure and displays the WordArt toolbar, as shown in this graphic:

CUSTOMIZING A WORDART OBJECT

Your new WordArt object could use some adjustment so that it fits under the right panel's bulleted dots. Also, you might want to experiment with the different styles that you can use to make your WordArt object more aptly fit your brochure's design. Let's customize the WordArt object:

1. Click **Rulers** on the **View** menu to display the rulers.

2. Double-click the WordArt toolbar's title bar to dock it out of the way.

3. Using the rulers as guides, drag the WordArt object's handles to reduce its size to approximately 1 inch tall by 2 inches wide.

4. Center the object under the row of dots in the brochure's right panel, and position it approximately halfway between the row of dots and the logo.

The results appear as shown in this graphic:

MORE WORDART OPTIONS

The WordArt toolbar has a variety of buttons for customizing your WordArt objects. You can use the Format WordArt features to add and modify borders, designate specific size settings, and perform other formatting tasks. Some of the text effects that you can apply by clicking the buttons on the WordArt toolbar include equalizing the height of the uppercase and lowercase letters; changing the spacing between characters; rotating, flipping, and stretching the text; and adjusting the text wrapping and alignment.

5. Click the **WordArt Shape** button on the WordArt toolbar. Publisher displays this palette of options:

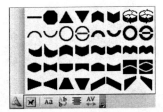

6. Experiment with some of the different shapes you can apply. When you are finished experimenting, click **Wave 1** (the fifth shape in the third row).

Publisher adjusts the text to display it in the wave shape.

7. Next click the **Format WordArt** button on the WordArt toolbar.

Publisher displays the Format WordArt dialog box shown in this graphic:

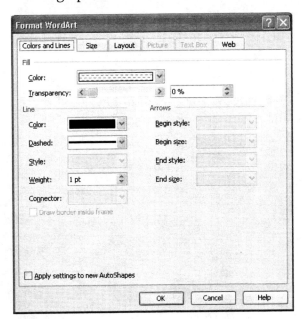

8. With the **Colors and Lines** tab displayed, click the **Color** down arrow in the **Fill** area, and then click the red color box (**Accent 3**, or the fourth box in the colors row) to coordinate the WordArt text color with the publication's color scheme.

9. Click **OK** to close the dialog box and apply the new color.

   The WordArt text looks a little squished.

10. Drag the middle-left handle .5 inch to the left and the middle-right handle .5 inch to the right.

    Now the WordArt object is approximately 3 inches wide and still centered under the dots.

11. Click anywhere outside the WordArt frame to close the WordArt toolbar, and then save your work.

    The Mojave Desert Jeep Tours title should look similar to the one shown in this graphic:

WORKING WITH TEMPLATE TABLES

When you first created the Adventure Works brochure, you based it on the Price List Brochure design. The price list brochure template includes ready-made tables with placeholders that you can replace to quickly create a price list. Tables might not be as exciting as fancy text and graphics, but they are an important visual element that you can use to lay out information in an easy-to-understand format. In this topic, you learn how to fill in a template table and how to modify a table to meet a specific need.

MODIFYING A TABLE TITLE

Let's start by modifying the Price List table title found on the brochure's second page:

1. Move to page 2 of the brochure, and scroll the top of the middle panel (which contains the Price List table and its title) into view.

2. Click an insertion point to the left of the *Price List* title placeholder, and type the word *Tour*, followed by a space.

3. Press **End** to move to the right end of the title, press **Enter**, and type *(Rates are per person)*, making sure to include the parentheses.

4. Select the second line of the title, and change its font size to **9**.

MODIFYING TABLE TEXT

The table in the middle panel of the brochure has two columns and eight rows. The intersection of each column and row, called a *cell*, is a field that can contain an item of information. In this exercise, you'll add information to the table's cells, using an easy method to move from cell to cell. Try this:

1. Move the mouse pointer over a blank area of the first *List your product or service here* cell.

    Publisher's ScreenTips feature indicates that you are now working in a table, as shown in this graphic:

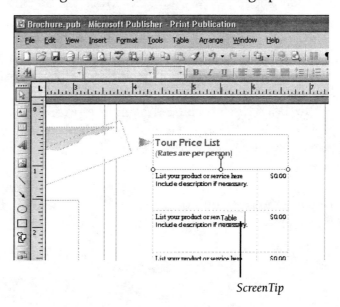

ScreenTip

2. In the first cell, select the **List your product or service here** placeholder text, and type *Two-Hour Mojave Desert Highlights Tour*.

   Notice that as you reach the right edge of the cell, the text automatically wraps to the next line.

3. Select the description placeholder text, and press the **Delete** key to remove it.

4. To move to the next cell in the same row of the table, press **Tab**.

   Publisher highlights the price placeholder.

5. Type *$45.00*, and press **Tab** to move to the first cell of the second row.

6. Continue filling in the price list by typing the entries shown below, pressing **Tab** to move from cell to cell:

Half-Day Joshua Tree National Park Tour	*$55.00*
Half-Day Old Woman Mountains Tour	*$65.00*
Half-Day Turtle Mountains Tour	*$65.00*
Full-Day Providence Mountains Tour	*$95.00*
Week-Long Death Valley National Park Tour	*$495.00*
Week-Long Mojave Desert Fossil Dig Tour	*$610.00*

   Pressing Shift+Tab moves the insertion point to the previous cell, and you can also use the Arrow keys and the mouse to move around.

REBREAKING LINES IN A TABLE

Publisher breaks lines in table cells to suit the width of the cell, not the sense of the cell entry. You might want to rebreak the lines in some of the cells to make their text easier to read. Follow these steps:

1. In the first cell of the first row, click an insertion point to the left of the word *Highlights*, and press **Shift+Enter**.

   Publisher moves the entire word to the second line.

2. In the first cell of the second row, click an insertion point to the left of the word *National*, and press **Shift+Enter**.

3. Repeat the previous step to move the word *Mountains* to the second line in the third, fourth, and fifth rows.

4. Use this line-breaking technique to move *National* in the sixth row and *Fossil* in the seventh row to their respective second lines.

5. Click anywhere outside the table.

The results are shown in this graphic:

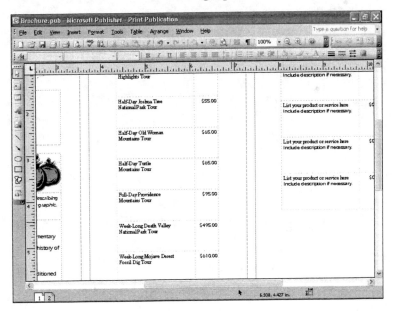

DELETING A TABLE ROW

You don't need the last row in the price list table. Here's how to delete it:

1. Click the table to select it.

2. Point to just outside the edge of the table to the left of the last row, and when the pointer changes to a black hoizontal arrow, click once to select the row.

3. Click **Delete** and then **Rows** on the **Table** menu.

FORMATTING A TABLE COLUMN

As you can see, the font of the entries in the first row of the table doesn't match the font in the rest of the brochure. You can change the font in the entire column, by following a couple of easy steps:

1. Click anywhere in the tours list, and click **Select** and then **Column** on the **Table** menu to select the entire column.

2. Change the font of the entire column's text by clicking the **Font** down arrow and clicking **Arial Black**.

DELETING A TABLE

You want only one table in the brochure, so you need to delete the table on the third panel. When you delete an element that occupies as much space as this table, you need to fill the space with something else, to avoid disrupting the design. In this case, you will use a title from the first panel of the brochure and a text paragraph from the flyer you created in Chapter 2. Follow these steps:

1. With the right panel in view, click the table's edge to select it, right-click it, and click **Delete Object** on the shortcut menu.

2. Scroll the left panel into view, click the **More About Our Tours** text box to select it, and click the **Copy** button on the Standard toolbar.

3. Scroll back to the third panel, click the **Paste** button, and move the title's text box so that it top-aligns with the text box of the table's title in the second panel.

4. Select the title text, type *Unbeatable Offer*, and then widen the text box.

   Make the text box as wide and high as the one shown in this graphic:

INFORMATION ABOUT
Using ruler guides to size and align, page 53

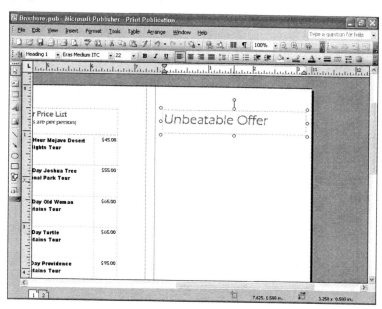

5. Repeat steps 2 and 3 to copy and paste the main text paragraph text box from the left panel to the right panel. Then move the text box below and adjoining the *Unbeatable Offer* title, and align the two text boxes.

6. Press **Ctrl+A** to select all the text in the text box, press the **Delete** key, and save your work.

7. Now open the **Flyer** publication, select the paragraphs and bulleted list in the second column of the main text area text box, and click the **Copy** button.

8. Close the flyer, paste the paragraph into the new text box on page 2 of the brochure, and replace the word *flyer* in the first paragraph by typing *brochure*.

9. Press **Ctrl+A**, and change the font size of the new text to **9**.

   The results are shown in this graphic:

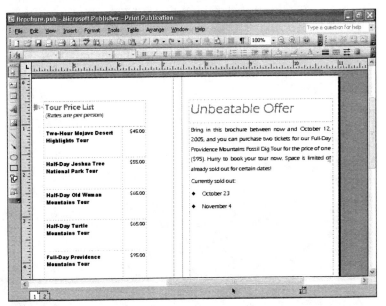

10. Scroll to the address text box at the bottom of the right panel, and change the font size to **9**.

11. Select all the text in the phone/fax/e-mail text box, change the font size to **9**, and then resize the text box to show all its text, including the web address.

WORKING WITH GRAPHICS

Publisher comes with a collection of ready-made graphics, called *clip art*, that are suitable for many different types of publications. In this topic, you'll use a couple of these clip art images in the brochure so that you can see how easy it is to import graphics into your publications.

REPLACING A PLACEHOLDER GRAPHIC

The left panel of page 2 of the brochure includes a placeholder graphic of tomatoes, with a placeholder caption. Follow these steps to replace this graphic with a more appropriate one:

1. Scroll to the left panel on page 2, and click the graphic placeholder (the tomatoes) to select it.

   Publisher selects both the graphic and its caption because they are grouped together.

2. Double-click the tomatoes graphic to display the **Clip Art** task pane, and then click the **Organize clips** link in the area at the bottom of the task pane.

   The Microsoft Clip Organizer stores folders containing hundreds of graphics organized in categories in the Collection List. (You can also find video and audio files in these folders.)

3. When the Clip Organizer window appears, click the plus sign to the left of the **Office Collections** folder.

   The Office Collections category appears in the Collection List, and the screen now appears as shown in this graphic:

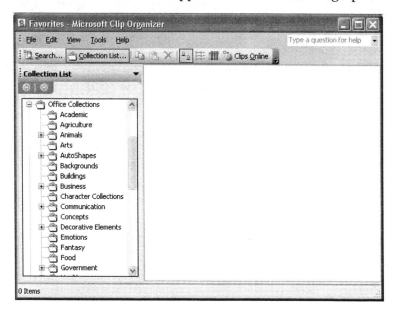

4. Scroll almost to the bottom of the **Office Collections** list, and click the **Weather** folder.

The right pane displays thumbnails of the graphics that belong to the Weather category, as shown in this graphic:

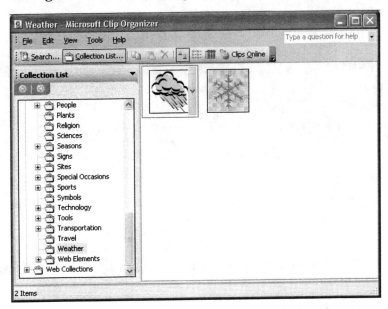

The two choices available for Weather don't really seem appropriate for an adventure travel brochure, so let's look in another area of the Clip Organizer.

INSERTING SCANNED IMAGES

Scanning an image stores a digital representation of the image as a graphics file. You can then insert it into a publication and move, resize, and crop it just like any other graphics file. If a scanner is attached to your computer, you can insert a scanned image into a publication directly from the scanner. (See Publisher's Help feature for more information.) If you don't have a scanner, you can take photographs or other images to a copy center or photo lab to have them scanned and then insert the resulting graphics file.

INSERTING GRAPHICS FROM OTHER SOURCES

To insert a graphics file from a source other than the Clip Organizer, click the Picture Frame button on the Objects toolbar, and with the resulting cross-hair pointer, draw a frame where you want the picture. When you release the mouse button, the Insert Picture dialog box appears. Browse to the graphics file you want, and double-click the file to insert it. Publisher can import a variety of graphics formats; look in the "Files of type" drop-down list in the Insert Picture dialog box to see them.

OTHER GRAPHIC OPTIONS

When you click a graphic's arrow to drop down its menu, the commands available allow you to preview the selected graphic in a separate window and examine its properties, make a copy of the clip available Offline, add it to the Favorites category or any other folder on your computer, and find clips of a similar type. In addition, you can edit the clip's keywords (the terms that describe each clip and that enable you to search for clips related to a specific topic).

5. Click the plus sign to the left of the **Web Collections** folder, and then if necessary, click the plus sign to the left of the **Microsoft Office Online** folder.

6. Scroll down the **Microsoft Office Online** list, and click the **Weather** folder.

    As you can see in this graphic, the Weather category in the Microsoft Office Online folder offers many more choices:

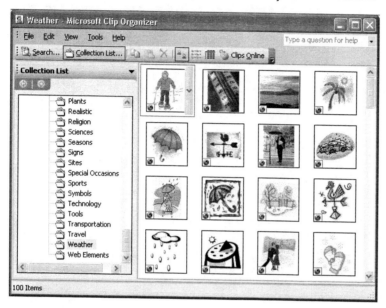

7. Scroll through the Weather graphics, point to the orange sun, and click the arrow that appears to the graphic's right.

    The menu shown in this graphic appears:

ACCESSING WEB COLLECTIONS

You must have an active Internet connection in order to view the large collection of graphics available for download from Microsoft Office Online or any other Web Collection.

8. Click **Copy** on the menu, and then close the Clip Organizer window by clicking its **Close** button. When Publisher asks whether you want to keep the copied graphic on the Clipboard, click **Yes**.

9. Select the tomatoes graphic, right-click it, and then click **Paste** to replace the tomatoes with the sun.

The brochure now looks as shown in this graphic:

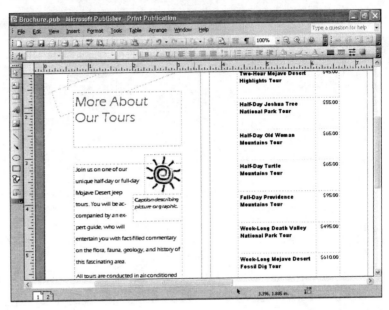

10. To give the new graphic a caption, select the caption placeholder and type *Enjoy clear skies and sunshine almost year-round*.

PLACING GRAPHICS ANYWHERE

Many of Publisher's templates include graphic placeholders that you can double-click and replace with graphics that are appropriate to your content. If you want to add a graphic to a page that doesn't have a placeholder, click the Picture Frame button on the Objects toolbar and then click Clip Art to open the Clip Art task pane. You can then find an appropriate graphic and insert it where you want. After you insert a graphic, you can move, resize, or customize it as usual.

ADDING CLIPS TO CLIP ORGANIZER

The first time you display the Clip Art task pane, Publisher might display the Add Clips to Organizer dialog box, asking if you want to catalog your media files. If you click the Now button, Publisher scans your hard drive for picture, sound, and movie files, and adds any files it finds to the Clip Organizer so that you can insert them as you would any other clip art files. To specify the folders you want Publisher to search in, click the Options button in the Add Clips to Organizer dialog box, select the check boxes of the folders you want, and then click Catalog. If you'd rather not catalog any files at this time, click the Later button in the Add Clips to Organizer dialog box. (To keep the dialog box from reappearing, select the "Don't show this message again" check box.) You can go back at any time. Click "Organize clips" in the Clip Art task pane to open the Clip Organizer dialog box. On the File menu, click Add Clips to Organizer, and then click Automatically. Select the option to add clips on your own if you want to add only one or two to specific folders you designate.

SEARCHING FOR A GRAPHIC

When you first opened the Clip Organizer, you might have noticed the Search button. Graphics stored in the Clip Organizer have one or more descriptive terms, called *keywords,* associated with them. Rather than scroll through the hundreds of graphics in the Clip Organizer, you can click the Search button and enter a keyword or two in the "Search for" box to locate a specific clip art graphic, and then click the Go button. You can also search for clips directly in the Clip Art task pane, without opening the Clip Organizer window. In this procedure, you'll use the Clip Art task pane to look for a graphic that represents fossils, and insert it on the left panel of the brochure's first page. Let's get going:

1. With the **Clip Art** task pane still open, move to the left panel of page 1, scroll the grapes graphic placeholder into view, click the graphic to select it and its caption, and then click the graphic a second time.

   The graphic's handles appear as dark gray circles.

2. Click an insertion point in the **Search for** box, type *fossils,* and click **Go**.

   The results are shown in this graphic:

If the results of a search don't identify a graphic you can use, you can enter a different word in the "Search for" box.

DISPLAYING A GRAPHIC'S KEYWORDS

To see a list of all the keywords attached to a graphic, you can click the graphic's arrow in the Clip Art task pane, click Edit Keywords on the drop-down menu, and examine the "Keywords for current clip" list on the Clip by Clip tab of the Keywords dialog box.

3. Click the animal skull graphic (the first graphic in the second row).

Publisher replaces the grapes with the animal skull graphic.

4. Scroll the brochure's right panel into view, and click the sunflowers graphic placeholder to select it. Then repeat steps 2 and 3 to search for and insert a new graphic using the keyword *desert*.

We chose one of the desert scenes farther down in the second column.

5. Close the **Clip Art** task pane.

At 66% magnification, the results appear as shown in this graphic:

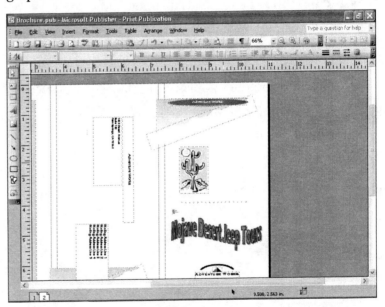

FINDING SIMILAR CLIPS

If you see a graphic with a style you like in the Clip Organizer window or the Clip Art task pane's search results, you can click the graphic's arrow and then click Find Similar Style on the menu. Publisher then displays graphics drawn in the same style as the selected graphic.

SEARCHING FOR CLIPS ONLINE

If you are connected to the Internet, you can click the "Clip art on Office Online" link at the bottom of the Clip Art task pane to access additional clips available on Microsoft's web site. After you click "Clip art on Office Online," Publisher starts your web browser and connects you to the Microsoft Clip Art and Media web site. Browse the categories on the page to search for and download a graphic that suits your needs. Select the check box below the graphic you want to add to your Selection Basket. When you finish making selections, click the link to download the items to a folder on your computer, ready to be cataloged by the Clip Organizer.

SIZING AND POSITIONING A GRAPHIC

Like other objects in Publisher, you can easily size and move clip art graphics in a publication. Follow these steps to reposition the desert graphic and change the size and location of the fossil graphic:

1. Check that the desert graphic is still selected, and then drag it to the right until it is approximately centered over the row of dots.

2. Scroll the brochure's left panel into view, and click the fossil graphic to select it.

3. Point to the fossil graphic's upper-right handle, and when the pointer changes to a double-headed arrow, drag up and to the right to increase both the height and width about .5 inch.

4. Next drag the graphic to the right until the right edges of both the graphic frame and caption text box are aligned with the right edges of the text boxes above and below them.

5. With the fossil graphic and its caption selected, click **Nudge** and then **Right** on the **Arrange** menu.

   Publisher nudges the graphic and its caption a tiny bit to the right.

6. Repeat step 5, nudging right or left as required until the right edges of the graphic frame and caption text box are exactly aligned with the right edges of the other text boxes on the panel.

7. Click the caption placeholder to select it, press **Ctrl+A** if necessary to select all the text, and type *Adventure Works is the only company offering fossil digs in the Mojave Desert.*

FLOWING TEXT AROUND GRAPHICS

By default, text flows around a graphic using the Square wrapping style, which fits any text surrounding the graphic around the graphic's square frame. To have text flow around the graphic with a different wrapping style, select the graphic, and click the Text Wrapping button on the Picture toolbar to drop down a list of text wrapping styles. The Tight option wraps the text tightly around the actual graphic, instead of its frame. The Through option allows the text to flow behind and be visible through the graphic. The Top and Bottom option wraps the text above and below the graphic, with no text to the right or left of it. Finally, the None option removes all text wrapping so that the graphic sits on top of and obscures the text.

8. Center the caption, rebreak the first line to the left of *is*, and rebreak the third line to the left of *Mojave*.

9. Click outside the graphic to deselect it.

   The results are shown in this graphic, at 75% magnification:

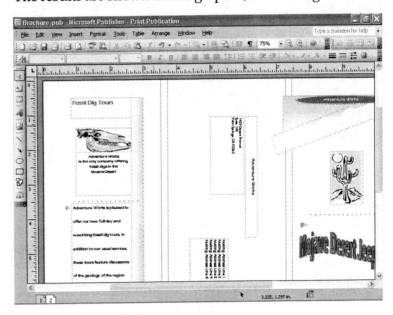

CHANGING A GRAPHIC'S COLOR

As you recall, you already added a logo to the right panel of the brochure. However, you still need to replace the logo's graphic placeholder and then make sure the graphic has a coordinating color. Follow these steps:

CROPPING GRAPHICS

To display only part of a graphic, make the graphic's frame smaller without scaling the graphic so that the part you don't want is hidden, or cropped. To crop ½ inch off the right side of the desert graphic, select the graphic and then click Picture on the Format menu to display the Picture tab of the Format Picture dialog box. In the "Crop from" area, type 0.5 in the Right box, and then click OK. Or click the Crop button on the Picture toolbar, point to a handle around the graphic, and drag to crop.

SCALING GRAPHICS

When you change the size of a graphic's frame, Publisher scales the graphic to fit the new frame size. You can also scale a graphic to a specific percentage (for example, 50% of its current size), and Publisher resizes the frame accordingly. To scale a graphic, select it, click Picture on the Format menu, click the Size tab in the Format Picture dialog box, enter a percentage in the Height or Width box in the Scale area, and click OK. (If you select the "Relative to original picture size" check box and then enter a percentage in the Height or Width box, Publisher enters the same value in the other box for you so that the picture's height and width remain relatively the same.) Click OK to close the Format Picture dialog box and apply the scaling changes to the graphic.

1. Zoom to **200%**, and scroll the logo at the bottom of the right panel into view. Then double-click the graphic placeholder (the pyramid) to open the **Clip Art** task pane.

2. In the **Search for** box, type *compasses*, and then click **Go**.

3. When Publisher displays the search results, find and click the stylized black-and-white compass symbol.

   Publisher replaces the pyramid graphic with the compass clip, as shown in this graphic:

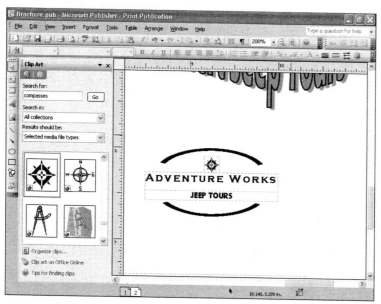

GRAPHIC COLORING OPTIONS

You can adjust the color of a graphic in several ways. On the Picture tab of the Format Picture dialog box, you can click options in the Color drop-down list to change a picture to grayscale, pure black and white, or washout. (Washout causes a graphic to appear like a watermark.) You can also drag the Brightness and Contrast sliders to adjust a graphic's brightness or contrast, which are set to 50% by default. In the Recolor Picture dialog box, you can choose to recolor an entire picture, as we've shown you, by clicking the desired option in the Color drop-down list. If none of the colors in the list appeals to you, click More Colors to display the Colors dialog box, where you can choose from an expanded color palette or create your own custom color. You can also recolor only the colored portions of the graphic, leaving the black portions as they are, by selecting the "Leave black parts black" option. If you don't like your changes and want to restore a graphic to its original appearance, click the Restore Original Colors button.

GRAPHIC BORDERS

Some Clip Organizer graphics come with borders around them and some don't. To surround a graphic (or any other object) with a border, select the graphic, click the Line/Border Style button on the Picture toolbar, and then make a selection from the available line and border styles. You can also click More Lines to display the Format Picture dialog box, and then click the Colors and Lines tab, customize the line appearance, and click OK.

4. Close the task pane, right-click the selected graphic, and click **Format Picture** on the shortcut menu.

5. When the Format Picture dialog box appears, make sure the **Picture** tab is displayed, and then click the **Recolor** button.

The Recolor Picture dialog box appears, as shown in this graphic:

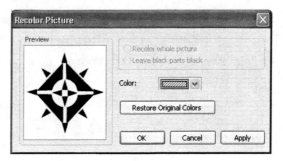

6. Click the **Color** down arrow, and then click the **Blue** box.

Publisher changes the graphic's color in the Preview box so that you can see the effects of your change.

7. Try the other colors, finishing up by clicking the **Red** box in the **Color** drop-down list.

8. Click **OK** twice to close the two dialog boxes.

WORKING WITH SHAPES

So far you have used only a few of the buttons on the Objects toolbar. In this topic, you'll learn how to use some of its other tools in order to draw shapes. You can add a shape to any publication and then adjust its appearance and location until it looks just the way you want it.

USING BORDERART

You can use BorderArt to put a graphical border around a text or picture frame. Select the text box or graphic, click the Line/Border Style button on the Formatting toolbar, and click More Lines. In the Format Picture or Format Text Box dialog box, click the BorderArt button on the Colors and Lines tab. In the BorderArt dialog box, select a border graphic from the Available Borders list, viewing the effects in the Preview pane on the right. If none of the styles fits your needs, click the Create Custom button to select a border graphic from the Clip Organizer window or another source. (Only simple graphics are candidates for BorderArt.) Give the new custom border a name, and click OK to add it to the Available Borders list. (You can also delete or rename any border in the list by selecting it and clicking the appropriate button.) When you have selected the border you want, click OK twice to apply it to your selected frame.

You can use ovals, rectangles, lines, and arrows to create custom shapes, but be sure to check the Design Gallery before doing this, because the shape you need might already be available.

DRAWING A SHAPE

You want to create a starburst shape to draw attention to the new Adventure Works fossil dig tours. Try this:

1. Press F9 to zoom the brochure to actual size, and then scroll the fossil graphic in the left panel into view.

2. Click the **AutoShapes** button on the Objects toolbar to display a menu of shape categories.

3. On the menu, click **Stars and Banners** to display a palette of star and banner shape options.

4. Click the **Explosion 1** shape (the first shape in the first row), and move the pointer over the publication.

5. Position the cross-hair pointer so that the pointer guides sit at the .5-inch mark on the horizontal ruler and the 1.5-inch mark on the vertical ruler.

6. Drag down and to the right until the shape is about 1 inch by 1 inch.

WORKING WITH A GROUP OF SHAPES

All the elements of a publication—text boxes, graphics, shapes, and so on—are *objects*. When you want to be able to move, resize, or rotate two or more objects simultaneously, you group them together. For example, suppose you want to add a text box in the middle of the starburst and then group the shape and the text box together so that you can rotate them both. Follow the steps on the next page.

ADDITIONAL SHAPES

If you hold down the Shift key while you are using the Line, Oval, or Rectangle button, you can draw straight horizontal or vertical lines, circles, or squares. To create an arrow, first draw one with the Arrow button on the Objects toolbar. Change the style of the arrow by clicking the Arrow Style button on the Formatting toolbar, and then clicking the arrow style you want on the drop-down palette. (You can choose from several different styles, including a left arrowhead, a right arrowhead, or both.) To fine-tune the arrow, click the Line/Border Style button, and then click More Lines to adjust the thickness, color, and arrow type on the Colors and Lines tab of the Format AutoShape dialog box. To remove an arrowhead, select the line, click the Arrow Style button, and click the line with no arrowhead at the top of the Arrow Styles palette.

1. Click the **Text Box** button on the Objects toolbar, and drag the cross-hair pointer to create a text box in the middle of the starburst.

2. With the insertion point in the new text box, type *New!*. Then change the font to **Eras Bold ITC**, and size the text to fit within the text box.

3. Select the starburst object by clicking one of its lines, and then add the text box to the selection by holding down the **Shift** key and clicking inside the text box.

   The selected objects look like this:

4. Click the **Group Objects** button attached to the selection to group the two objects.

   The objects are now surrounded by one set of handles, and it is no longer possible to move or resize the shape without moving or resizing the text, and vice versa.

5. Because the shape is a little too close to the fossil graphic, drag the grouped object slightly down and to the left.

   Both the shape and the text move as a group to their new position. Now suppose you decide to reposition the text within the shape. To move just the text, you must first ungroup the objects.

6. Click the **Ungroup Objects** button, and then click outside the starburst to remove the selection.

7. Click the text box to select it, click **Nudge**, and then on the **Arrange** menu, click **Left** or **Right** as required to adjust the position of the text box.

8. Press the **Shift** key, click the starburst to add it to the selection, and then click the **Group Objects** button to group the objects again.

FLIPPING OBJECTS

To make an object face a different direction, you can flip it horizontally or vertically. Select the object, click the Free Rotate down arrow on the Standard toolbar, and then click Flip Horizontal or Flip Vertical on the drop-down menu. To quickly rotate an object 90 degrees in either direction, you can click Rotate Right 90 or Rotate Left 90 on the same drop-down menu. (The Free Rotate button changes to whatever Free Rotate command you last clicked, so if you want to repeat that command, you can just click the button.)

9. Point to the green rotate handle just above the upper-middle handle on the grouped object.

The mouse pointer changes to a rotate icon, as shown in this graphic:

10. Drag the rotate handle to the left until the shadow image tilts to about a 45-degree angle from the original graphic's placement, and click away from the group to deselect it.

The results look similar to those shown in this graphic:

CHANGING A SHAPE'S COLOR

You know how to recolor a graphic. You can recolor a shape in the same way. Here we'll show you how to recolor the shapes that are part of the logo by using the Format AutoShape dialog box, and then you'll quickly color the starburst using the Fill Color button. Follow these steps:

1. Scroll the logo at the bottom of the third panel into view, and then click the bottom curved line of the logo once to select it.

When the line is selected, gray handles appear around the object.

2. Double-click the bottom curved line.

The Colors and Lines tab of the Format AutoShape dialog box appears, as shown in the graphic on the next page.

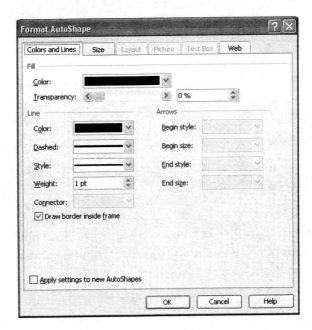

3. In the **Fill** area, click the **Color** down arrow, and then click
    the slate-blue color box (**Accent 1**, or the second box in the
    colors row).

4. In the **Line** area, click the **Color** down arrow, click the slate-
    blue color box (**Accent 1**), and click **OK**.

    You need to change both the fill and line colors for the
    curved lines to be colored uniformly.

5. Repeat the previous steps to change the top curved line's
    colors.

6. Select the **Adventure Works** text, click the **Font Color**
    down arrow on the Formatting toolbar, and click the slate-
    blue color box (**Accent 1**).

7. Repeat step 6 to recolor the **Jeep Tours** text.

    The logo is shown in this graphic:

8. Scroll to the starburst object on the first panel, and click it
    to select it.

9. Click the **Fill Color** down arrow on the Formatting toolbar, 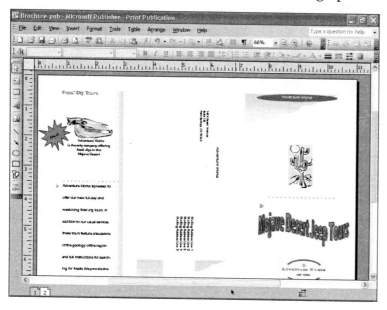 and then click the red color box (**Accent 3**, or the fourth box in the colors row) in the drop-down palette.

10. Click outside the object to deselect it.

HIDING AND DISPLAYING ON-SCREEN GUIDES

When you want to view the results of your work as it will appear when printed, you can hide the on-screen guides. Let's do that now so that you can get a clearer picture of what the completed brochure looks like:

1. Change the zoom percentage to **66%** to display more of the brochure.

2. Click **Boundaries and Guides** on the **View** menu to remove the command's check mark and turn it off.

Your brochure looks like the one shown in this graphic:

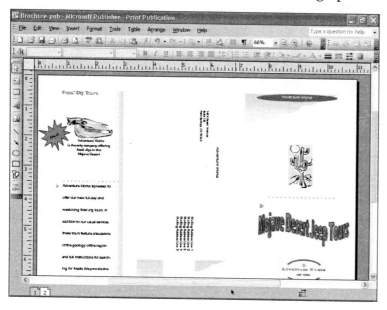

3. Click **Boundaries and Guides** on the **View** menu to turn the command back on and redisplay the on-screen guides for your next project.

4. If you want, click the **Print** button to see the results of your work on paper.

5. To get a better overview of the brochure's layout, place the two printed pages back to back, and fold the brochure into three panels.

6. Save and close the Brochure file.

PART TWO

BUILDING PROFICIENCY

In Part Two, you build on the skills you gained in the first half of the course. In Chapter 4, you learn design and editorial concepts as you create a newsletter. In Chapter 5, you develop a press release template with foreground and background layers and a custom color scheme. In Chapter 6, you take care of final details, including the proofing and page adjustments that will make your publications both attractive and accessible.

DESIGNING LONGER PUBLICATIONS

In Part One, you worked with several types of short publications and gained a good foundation in Publisher's basics. Because you created publications using Publisher's built-in design sets, you had to do very little design work. However, when you create longer publications, layout and editorial issues are much more important. For example, if a publication includes several stories, you must decide in what order to place them and how the text of each story should flow on each page. Depending on the type of publication, you might also need to incorporate graphics, tables, or forms into the publication. In this chapter, you create a monthly newsletter for Adventure Works. Even if you don't anticipate ever publishing a newsletter, you will be able to apply the concepts discussed in this chapter to any long publication, and once you feel comfortable, you can experiment on your own. (Often the most attention-grabbing designs break all the rules!)

When you have finished this chapter, you will know how to:

- Set up newsletters
- Make design decisions
- Work with text in longer publications
- Fill white space
- Create tables from scratch
- Work with forms

Create tables from scratch and then format them.

Use quote frames to add interest.

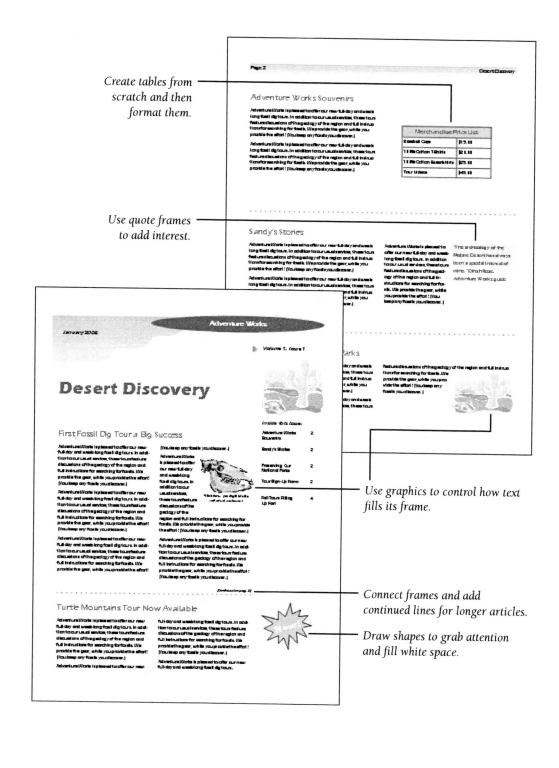

Use graphics to control how text fills its frame.

Connect frames and add continued lines for longer articles.

Draw shapes to grab attention and fill white space.

SETTING UP NEWSLETTERS

The first thing you need to do is create the newsletter that you will be working with in this chapter. In this topic, we show you how to set up the newsletter and adjust the basic page layout.

CREATING A NEWSLETTER BY USING A DESIGN SET

The easiest way to take the grunt work out of setting up a newsletter is to use one of Publisher's built-in design sets as a starting point. Follow these steps:

1. If necessary, start **Publisher**. If Publisher is already running, close any open publications, and make sure the **New Publication** task pane is displayed.

2. In the task pane's **New from a design** area, click **Publications for Print**, click **Newsletters**, and then in the **Newsletters** pane in the work area, click the **Waves Newsletter** thumbnail.

3. When the **Newsletter Options** task pane opens, make sure 2 is selected in the **One- or two-sided printing** area to designate a double-sided layout for the publication.

4. Click **Include** in the **Customer address** area to include a placeholder for a customer address.

INFORMATION ABOUT
Color schemes, page 26

5. Click the **Color Schemes** link at the top of the task pane, and notice that **Tropics** is already selected in the **Color Schemes** task pane's **Apply a color scheme** list.

   To help you maintain a consistent color scheme, Publisher has applied the color scheme you selected for previous publications. You can change the color scheme in this task pane if you want; however, for the purposes of this exercise, leave the color scheme set at Tropics.

ADJUSTING THE PAGE LAYOUT

Publisher has established a basic page layout for the newsletter, but you need to change it. You want to format the newsletter so that its text appears in two columns, and then you want to add a sign-up form. Follow these steps:

1. Click the **Newsletter options** link, and in the **Newsletter Options** task pane, click the **Page Content** link to display the **Page Content** task pane.

2. In the **Columns** area, click the down arrow to the right of the **2** option, and then click **Apply to All Pages**.

   Publisher applies a 2-column format to the entire newsletter.

3. Click the **2** button in the page navigation controls at the bottom of the window.

   The second and third pages of the newsletter are now displayed in the publication window. The Page Content task pane has changed to show options available for the newsletter's inside page content, as shown in this graphic:

4. Click the **Select a page to modify** down arrow, and click **Right inside page**.

5. In the **Content for Right Page** area, click the **Sign-up form** option to change the layout of the right page.

6. Click the task pane's **Close** button to allow more room for the newsletter.

The two inside pages now look as shown in this graphic:

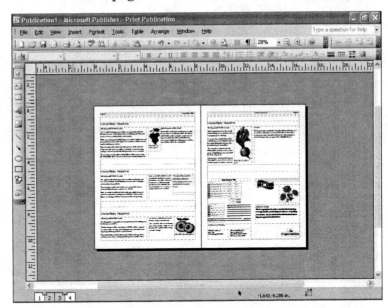

In the publishing world, two facing pages are called a *spread*. When you design longer publications, you will want to look at spreads to see how the pages balance.

7. Save the file in the My Documents folder as *Newsletter*.

Remember to save frequently from now on.

MAKING DESIGN DECISIONS

Before you begin making design decisions about the newsletter, you must first work out the details of its contents. Even though you can change elements later if they aren't working for you, it's best to have the most important issues ironed out beforehand. Here are some basic guidelines to follow when developing a longer publication:

- **The audience.** Determine the type of audience you are trying to attract so that you can make decisions about the tone, language level, and graphics you will use.

- **The content.** Decide what information you want to include, and which elements are most important.

- **The visual enhancements.** If you have several graphics available, determine which ones best enhance your stories.

TWO-PAGE VIEW

By default, Publisher displays a multi-page publication in two-page view. When you click the 2 button to move from page 1 to page 2 of the newsletter, Publisher displays pages 2 and 3—the next two-page spread. To display one page at a time, click Two-Page Spread on the View menu to turn off the command. But remember to closely scrutinize your two-page spreads for balance before sending them off to the printer.

DETERMINING WHO THE AUDIENCE IS

Before you spend time, and perhaps money, to get your message out to the world, it makes sense to know as much as possible about your target audience. Here are a few audience issues to consider:

- **Their ages.** How old are they? The answer to this question influences the reading level and language of your stories, but it is also a major consideration when you are determining how the newsletter should look.

- **Their needs.** Does what you have to offer meet a need, or does it satisfy a desire? The answer to this question determines whether your design and tone are straightforward and down-to-earth, or exciting and evocative.

- **Their characteristics.** Do your readers have common interests, opinions, hopes, or fears? The answer to this question influences the topics you discuss and how you discuss them. If you don't know the answer and you want to appeal to the broadest possible audience, you'll want to keep your discussions general and steer clear of controversial topics.

- **Their levels of interest.** Have your readers already indicated an interest in what you have to say? The answer to this question determines how persuasive the newsletter must be, and how quickly you must convince your readers that they should spend time reading it beyond the first headline.

- **Their levels of knowledge.** What do your readers already know about this topic in general and about your organization, service, or product in particular? The answer to this question has some bearing on the amount of space you will dedicate to background information and whether you can use jargon that might otherwise be unfamiliar to readers who have limited knowledge about the newsletter's subject matter.

By answering these and any other questions you can think of about your audience, you can focus your efforts so that your publications achieve the maximum results. For example, suppose you want to send the Adventure Works newsletter to all past customers, whose ages vary widely, who have taken at least one jeep tour for fun, who have demonstrated an interest in the desert, and who know about the company and its products. This newsletter would likely be quite different from one aimed at attracting senior citizens who have never taken a jeep tour

PRINTING OPTIONS

When making design decisions about your publications, you also need to consider your printing options, including type of paper, color or black ink, print quality, and so forth. If you are using a printing service, discuss these issues with your printer before you start work on a publication. Other features frequently requested when using a commercial printer include process-color (CMYK) composite postscript files and separations, which you can generate directly from the Print dialog box. See Publisher's Help for more information on how to prepare your publications for commercial printing.

before, who are concerned about their safety and comfort, who think deserts are sandy expanses devoid of plant and animal life, and who have never heard of Adventure Works.

DETERMINING WHAT'S MOST IMPORTANT

Armed with information about your audience, you can move on to decide which of the items slated for inclusion in the newsletter are most important and should appear most prominently. Suppose Adventure Works wants the newsletter to drum up repeat business, but also hopes it will generate some referrals. For the premiere issue, you decide to emphasize the new fossil dig tours by including a story about them on the front page to appeal to existing customers. You will also include information about the company's other tours, in case existing customers pass on the newsletter to potential new customers. Let's start by adding the information for the newsletter's masthead and a heading for the lead story, and then you'll allocate space for the other stories. Follow these steps:

1. Move to page 1, and change the zoom setting to **100%**.

2. Scroll to the top of the newsletter, click the **Newsletter Date** placeholder, select all the text by pressing **Ctrl+A** (if necessary), and type *January 2005*.

3. Select the **Adventure Works** text in the oval graphic, click the **Bold** button, click the **Font Size** down arrow, and then click **14** in the drop-down list.

    Now the company name clearly stands out on the front page.

4. Click the **Newsletter Title** placeholder, select all the text, and type *Desert Discovery*. Then change the title's font to **Eras Bold ITC** and its size to **36**.

5. Click the **Lead Story Headline** placeholder, select all the text, and type *First Fossil Dig Tour a Big Success*.

Here are the results:

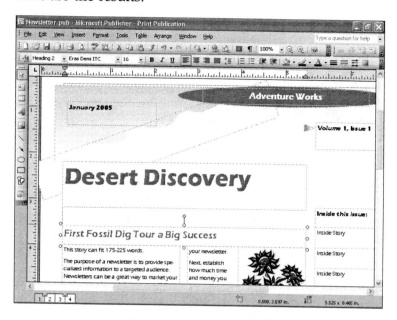

6. Scroll to the bottom of the first page, click the **Secondary Story Headline** placeholder, select all the text, and type *Turtle Mountains Tour Now Available*.

   Although you don't expect the Turtle Mountains tour to be as popular as the fossil dig tours, leave the text size and spacing of the heading the same as the lead story's for consistency. The story's lower position automatically makes it seem less important.

7. Click the **2** button in the page navigation controls to move to the inside spread, and then scroll up and to the left to display the top of page 2.

   Adventure Works sells shirts and hats, and you want to advertise them in a story at the top of this page.

8. Click the topmost **Inside Story Headline** placeholder, select all the text, and then type *Adventure Works Souvenirs* to replace the placeholder text.

9. Replace the text of the second **Inside Story Headline** placeholder with *Sandy's Stories*, and replace the text of the third headline placeholder with *Preserving Our National Parks*.

10. Scroll to page 3, and replace page 3's **Inside Story Headline** placeholder text with *Fossil Dig Tours*.

    The *Fossil Dig Tours* story that starts on page 1 will continue here.

11. Click the 4 button in the page navigation controls to move to page 4, scroll down, and replace the **Back Page Story Headline** placeholder text with *Fall Tours Filling Up Fast*.

DETERMINING WHICH GRAPHICS TO USE

You've taken care of all the story headlines. Now you need to decide which stories will have accompanying graphics or graphic elements and review the graphic placeholders Publisher has inserted for you. You will then have a good idea of the newsletter's potential layout before you add the text. Follow these steps:

1. Click the 1 button in the page navigation controls to move to the first page. Then zoom to 75%, and scroll through the page to get an overview of its layout.

   You want to keep all the elements on this page except the *Special points of interest* text box.

2. Right-click the **Special points of interest** text box, and click **Delete Object** on the shortcut menu.

3. Move to page 2, and delete the grapes graphic and caption accompanying the *Adventure Works Souvenirs* story.

   You want to allow space for a table that lists the available souvenirs and their prices.

4. Move to page 3, and delete the vegetable graphic and caption accompanying the continuation of the *Fossil Dig Tours* story.

   You now have only one graphic for the *Fossil Dig Tours* story, which appears with the beginning of the story on page 1. However, several graphic elements appear in the lower area of this page, including the logo, which is already featured on the back page. You don't need the logo here as well.

5. Click the logo to select it, and press the **Delete** key.

6. Save the publication.

WORKING WITH TEXT IN LONGER PUBLICATIONS

In short publications, you generally have only a few text elements to work with, and you don't have to worry too much about the way text flows and making everything fit. With longer publications, you have to juggle more elements, and if a story won't fit on one page, you have to ensure both that it continues on another page with no lost text and that the reader knows exactly where to find the continuation.

ENTERING AND FORMATTING TEXT

Before we can show you some techniques for manipulating text in a longer publication, you need to have some text to work with. In this case, you will use multiple copies of a paragraph from a publication you already created, instead of doing a lot of typing. You will also see how to quickly move through a story containing multiple text boxes and how to format copied text to match other text in the publication. Follow these steps:

1. Without closing the Newsletter publication, open the **Brochure** publication that you created in Chapter 3.

2. In the left panel of the first page, select the paragraph about fossil dig tours by clicking its text box and pressing **Ctrl+A**. Then click the **Copy** button on the Standard toolbar.

3. Redisplay the **Newsletter** publication, press **F9** to zoom to 100%, and move to the bottom of the first page.

4. Click the first text box of the two-column *Turtle Mountains* story, and with all the text selected, click the **Paste** button to replace the placeholder text with the paragraph from the brochure.

   As you can see, the paragraph retains its original formatting when you paste it. Publisher recognizes that the two text boxes of the *Turtle Mountains* story are connected, and assigns a Go to Previous Text Box button to the second column.

5. Click the **Go to Previous Text Box** button to move the selection to the first text box of the story, and then click the **Go to Next Text Box** button to move back to the second text box.

6. Press **Ctrl+A** to select the text of the newly inserted paragraph, click **Paragraph** on the **Format** menu to display the Paragraph dialog box.

7. On the **Indents and Spacing** tab, type *1.17* in the **Between lines** box, press **Tab**, type *6* in the **After paragraphs** box, click **OK**, and then click a blank area of the page to remove the text selection.

The results are shown in this graphic:

8. Select the text of the new paragraph again, click the **Copy** button to copy the paragraph with the correct formatting, press **End** to move the insertion point to the end of the selected paragraph, press **Enter**, and click the **Paste** button.

9. Press **Enter**, and click the **Paste** button again to insert the paragraph a third time.

Publisher displays the message box shown in this graphic, asking whether you want to have the text of the story automatically flowed into new text boxes:

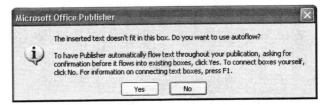

INFORMATION ABOUT

Flowing text, page 99

MARKING THE END OF STORIES

Newsletters and magazines often designate the ends of stories with a graphic character. This device is not only useful to the readers but to anyone proofreading your publications. The graphic element assures them that they have reached the end of the story and that no text is missing or located elsewhere. To add a graphic character, click an insertion point at the end of the story, and use the Symbol dialog box to insert a symbol.

INSERTING AND DELETING PAGES

To insert a new two-page spread in a multi-page publication, click Page on the Insert menu or press Ctrl+Shift+N to display the Insert Newsletter Pages dialog box. Then designate what you want to appear on the left and right pages by selecting options from drop-down lists. (You can add stories, calendars, and three types of forms.) Click the More button to display the Insert Pages dialog box, where you can insert new pages in a one-page publication, designating how many pages you want to insert and whether they should appear before or after the existing page. You can decide to insert a blank page, a page with a single text box that takes up the whole page, or a page that duplicates all objects on the existing page. There are also options for inserting just one page in a multi-page publication, rather than a spread. To delete a page, move to the page, click Delete Page on the Edit menu, and click OK to confirm the action.

10. Click **No** to return to the story.

Because not all of the story is visible, it has been assigned a Text in Overflow button.

11. Move to page 2, and replace the text of the *Adventure Works Souvenirs* story with two copies of the brochure paragraph, making sure to press **Enter** after each one to insert a blank line between them. Then replace the text of the *Sandy's Stories* story with three copies, and replace the text of the *Preserving Our National Parks* story with two copies.

12. Move to page 4, and replace the text of the final story of the newsletter with five copies of the paragraph.

EDITING TEXT IN MICROSOFT WORD

The paragraphs that represent the *Turtle Mountains* story are present in the newsletter, but not all of the story is visible. You have several options: You can increase the size of the story's text boxes; flow the text into an additional connected text box; or edit the text to make it fit the existing available space. You want to delete all but the first sentence of the final paragraph to make the paragraph fit in the text box. This is a relatively simple process, but for those times when more complicated editing is involved, it's good to know that you can switch to Microsoft Word to take advantage of its superior editing capabilities. Follow these steps to see how this works:

1. Right-click the second text box of the *Turtle Mountains* story on the first page, click **Change Text**, and then click **Edit Story in Microsoft Word**.

EDITING TEXT TO FIT IT INTO A TEXT BOX

To fit text in a text box, you can try eliminating extraneous words to decrease the number of lines or adding words to increase the number of lines. Depending on the type of text you are dealing with and whether you have the authority to make changes to it, you might consider the following:

- **Active vs. passive.** Active sentences are usually shorter than passive ones. For example, *We provide the gear* is one word shorter than *The gear will be provided.*
- **Words vs. phrases.** You can often expand words into phrases or contract phrases into words. For example, *the geology of the region* is two words longer than *the region's geology.*
- **Simple vs. compound structures.** You can often insert or delete adjectives or adverbs without changing meaning, and you can substitute shorter or longer words or interchange simple and compound verbs. For example, *Adventure Works is very pleased to be able to offer our exciting new full-day and week-long fossil dig tours* is five words longer than the equivalent sentence in the newsletter.

The text of the story appears as a Word document that you can edit the same as you would any other Word document.

2. Click an insertion point to the left of the second sentence in the final paragraph, hold down the **Shift** key, and press the **Down Arrow** key three times to select the last three sentences.

3. Press **Delete** to delete the selected sentences.

4. Click Word's **Close** button to close Word and return to the newsletter.

    The story now fits in its text box with no overflow.

FLOWING TEXT FROM TEXT BOX TO TEXT BOX

When placing longer stories in a multi-page publication, you will often need to start a story on one page and continue it on another. Because all text must be contained in a text box, you need to tell Publisher which text box to continue the text in. To add the text for the *Fossil Dig Tours* story on page 1 and continue the story on page 3 of the newsletter, follow these steps:

1. Move to page 1, scroll the *Fossil Dig Tours* story into view, select its placeholder text, and press **Delete**.

2. Click the **Paste** button to insert the paragraph you copied from the *Turtle Mountains* story, and then press **Enter**. Repeat this step four more times.

3. When Publisher displays the overflow text message box, click **No**.

    Before you can continue the *Fossil Dig Tours* story in the text box on page 3, you need to delete its placeholder text.

4. Move to page 3, select the text of the *Fossil Dig Tours* story, and press **Delete**.

5. Move back to page 1, click the second text box of the *Fossil Dig Tours* story to select it, and then click the **Create Text Box Link** button on the Connect Text Boxes toolbar.

    The pointer changes into a pitcher, indicating that you can now "pour" the story into a continuing text box.

6. Move back to page 3, and click the first text box designated as the continuation of the *Fossil Dig Tours* story.

Publisher connects the text boxes and inserts the text that overflows from the *Fossil Dig Tours* text box on page 1 into the text box on page 3, as shown in this graphic:

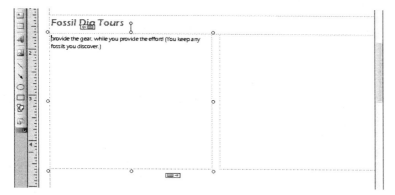

7. Click an insertion point at the end of the text, press **Enter**, and then paste the paragraph again. Repeat this step three more times to finish up the story.

8. With the story's last text box selected, click the **Go to Previous Text Box** button to move to the text box to the left of the selected text box.

9. Click the **Go to Previous Text Box** button again to move to the second text box of the story, which is on page 1 of the newsletter.

ADDING "CONTINUED" LINES

Suppose you want to add "continued" lines to the *Fossil Dig Tours* story to let the readers know on which pages the story begins and ends. Follow these steps:

1. With the second text box of the *Fossil Dig Tours* story selected on the first page of the newsletter, right-click the text text box, and click **Format Text Box** on the shortcut menu.

    The Format Text Box dialog box appears.

2. Click the **Text Box** tab, select the **Include "Continued on page…"** check box below the **Text autofitting** area, and click **OK**.

DISCONNECTING TEXT BOXES

To disconnect two text boxes, click the first text box and then on the Connect Text Boxes toolbar click the Break Forward Link button. The second text box is then removed from the chain, and the text it contained is placed back in the text overflow area. You can then pour the text somewhere else by connecting its text box to another text box, or you can make the first text box large enough to display all of it.

The results are shown in this graphic:

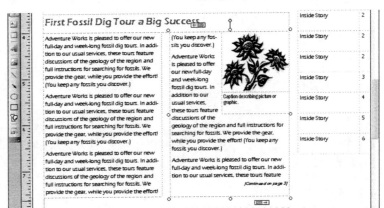

Notice that you don't have to enter a page number. Because the text boxes are connected, Publisher knows that the story continues on page 3. Also notice that by adding this line to the selected text box, you have bumped one line of text to page 3. The second text box would look better with one more line to balance the two "columns."

3. Drag the second text box's lower-middle handle downward to make the text box large enough to move the displaced line of text back onto the first page.

4. Click the **Go to Next Text Box** button to move to page 3.

5. Right-click the first text box in the *Fossil Dig Tours* story on that page, and then click **Format Text Box**.

6. Click the **Text Box** tab, select the **Include "Continued from page…"** check box, and click OK.

This time, Publisher adds a line to the top of the selected text box, as shown in this graphic:

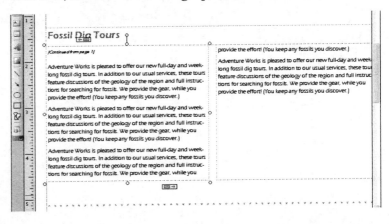

FILLING WHITE SPACE

After entering all the text of a longer publication, you can begin to juggle the other elements. In the publishing world, the blank areas of a page are known as *white space*. If you crowd too many different items of information together, your message can get lost, so a well-designed publication uses a certain amount of white space to visually separate the items. However, using too much white space can make a publication look empty, boring, unbalanced, or all three! Let's take a closer look at each page of the newsletter and add visual elements where they will enhance its overall appearance.

ADDING GRAPHICS TO THE NEWSLETTER

You notice that there is too much white space on the first page of the newsletter. Let's fix it by adding a couple of graphics to catch the reader's eye:

1. Move to page 1, and zoom to **33%** so that you can see the entire page at a glance.

   The first two columns are filled with text, but the last column contains too much white space.

2. Press **F9**, scroll to the top of the page, and make sure that the rulers are turned on.

3. Click the **Picture Frame** button on the Objects toolbar, and then click **Clip Art**.

4. In the **Clip Art** task pane, make sure **All collections** appears in the **Search in** box. Then in the **Search for** box, type *desert* and click **Go** to search for the desert graphic you used in the brochure.

5. Click a desert graphic in the search results to insert the graphic on page 1, and then resize and reposition the graphic so that it measures 1.25 inches high by 1.75 inches wide and is located directly below the *Volume 1, Issue 1* text box.

6. If necessary, use the **Nudge** command on the **Arrange** menu to fine-tune the placement of the graphic so that its frame is left-aligned with the text in the frames above and below it.

   INFORMATION ABOUT
   Nudging graphics, page 99

7. Click the sunflower graphic adjacent to the *First Fossil Dig Tour a Big Success* story twice to select it, search for *fossils* in the **Clip Art** task pane, and click the animal skull picture you used in the brochure. Close the **Clip Art** task pane, and reposition and resize the graphic as necessary.

8. Replace the caption text below the graphic with *Who knows…
    you might find the remains of a dinosaur!* Then click the
    Center button on the Formatting toolbar to center the cap-
    tion under the graphic.

    The results are shown in this graphic:

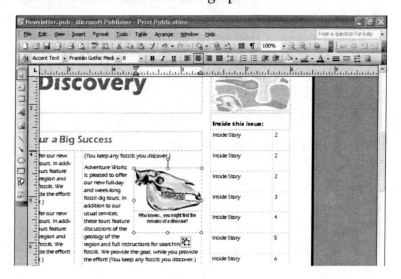

INSERTING AN ATTENTION GETTER

Sometimes, newsletters include little announcements or re-
minders that can easily get lost if they are presented as ordinary
text. This type of element is a good candidate for an attention
getter—a message presented with splash of color or inside a
shape so that it catches the eye. Attention getters can also be
used to fill areas of white space that don't warrant the use of a
graphic or other object. Let's fill the white space at the bottom
of the right column with an appealing attention getter:

1. Scroll to the lower-right corner of page 1. Then click the
    Design Gallery Object button on the Objects toolbar, click
    the **Attention Getters** category, and double-click the **Explo-
    sion Attention Getter** thumbnail to insert it on page 1.

2. Move the object into the white space to the right of the
    Turtle Mountains story, and click outside the object to de-
    select it.

3. Click inside the **2 for 1** text box to highlight all the text, and
    type *New!*

4. Double-click the object outside the text box to display the
    Format Object dialog box, click the **Size** tab, type *345* in the
    Rotation box of the **Size and rotate** area, and click **OK**.

5. Click the **Fill Color** down arrow on the Formatting toolbar, and click the gold color box (**Accent 2** third box in the colors row) to change the object's color.

   The text box has a black border around it that you don't want.

6. Double-click the text box to display the Format Text Box dialog box. Then in the **Line** area, click the **Color** down arrow, click **No Line** in the drop-down list, and then click **OK**.

7. Resize the object so that it fills up more of the white space next to the *Turtle Mountains* story.

   The results are shown in this graphic:

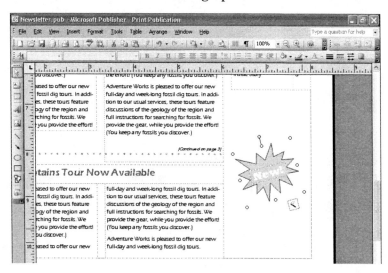

   This Design Gallery object helps draw the reader's attention to a story that might otherwise get lost at the bottom of the page. The object's color is subdued, but because it's not crowded by other objects, it pops out on the page.

FINE-TUNING THE NEWSLETTER'S CONTENT

You want to make a few more adjustments to the newsletter so that it looks just right. You'll update the text of a quote text box, replace placeholder clip art with a graphic appropriate to this publication, and then move and size a few frames and text boxes until everything looks balanced. Follow these steps:

1. Move to pages 2 and 3, change the zoom setting to 33%, and scroll the window so that you can see the two-page spread.

   The most glaring area of white space is next to the first story, but this space is reserved for a table, which will balance nicely with the form at the bottom of page 3. The items on page 2 that need your attention are the boxed quote and the graphic that accompanies the last story.

2. Press **F9**, click the quote text box on page 2, select all its text, and type *"The archaeology of the Mojave Desert has always been a special interest of mine." Dinah Soar, Adventure Works guide*.

3. Scroll down to the *Preserving Our National Parks* story on page 2, double-click the peach placeholder graphic to open the **Clip Art** task pane, and search for and insert a suitable replacement. When you have finished, close the task pane.

We used the desert scene again.

4. Delete the new graphic's caption text, but not the caption text box.

5. Drag the lower-middle handle of the first text box of the story upward until *feature discussions* appears at the top of the second text box. Then move and resize the graphic until it is aligned with the quote box in the preceding story.

The results are shown in this graphic:

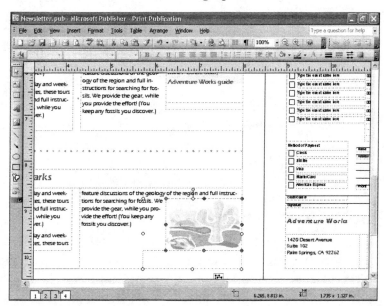

PULL QUOTES

A quote text box, or pull quote, is a good way to fill white space and draw the eye toward a story. To create one from scratch, click the Design Gallery Object button on the Objects toolbar, click the Pull Quotes category in the Categories list, and then double-click a pull quote thumbnail to insert it in your publication. You can then move and size it as you would any other text box.

As you can see, you can experiment with the size of text boxes and objects to force text to rewrap, thereby filling white space and balancing the page.

6. Scroll to page 3, and replace the sunflower graphic to the right of the form with a graphic that is appropriate for the Adventure Works newsletter. When you have finished, close the task pane.

We chose the animal skull graphic again.

RECYCLING A LOGO

You need to update the logo on page 4 so that it is appropriate for the newsletter. Follow the steps below:

1. Move to page 4, and scroll to the top of the page.

2. Select the **Organization** text box and its grouped logo, and delete it.

3. Save the **Newsletter** file (clicking **No** if Publisher asks if you want to apply the logo deletion to the business information set), and then if necessary, open **Brochure**.

4. Copy the **Adventure Works** logo from the third panel of the brochure, redisplay **Newsletter**, and paste the logo on page 4.

5. Move the logo to the upper-left corner, directly below the **Adventure Works** text box, and adjust its size until its text box is the same width as the one below it and all its text is visible.

6. Scroll down to the oval object advertising the web address, replace the oval's text with *Check out our web site at www.adworks.tld*, and then drag the object's lower-right handle downward and to the right until all its text is visible.

7. Move the oval object downward so that its information does not get lost below the address and phone text boxes.

8. Replace the peach graphic in the lower-right corner of the page with a graphic appropriate for the adjacent story. Then close the **Clip Art** task pane, position and size the graphic so that the text rewraps in a skinny column to its left, and delete the graphic's caption text.

We used the cactus with the big sun. The results are shown at 40% magnification in the graphic on the next page.

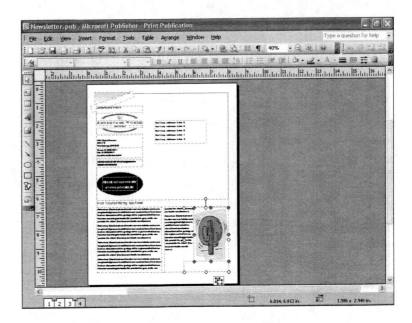

CREATING TABLES FROM SCRATCH

We've already shown you how to fill in a pre-existing table. Now we'll show you how to create a table from scratch.

INSERTING A NEW TABLE

To demonstrate how easy the process is, we'll show you how to create a table that lists the souvenir merchandise sold by Adventure Works. Follow these steps:

WORKING WITH TABS

Many tables are simple tabular lists that align information in columns. To use tabs to create a table, enter the text you want to appear in the first column, and press the Tab key to move to the next column. The insertion point jumps to a position that corresponds to that of the next tab setting. By default, Publisher sets tabs at every half inch. To adjust the position of the default tabs, click Tabs on the Format menu, and change the "Default tab stops" setting. To set a custom tab using this dialog box, enter the tab's position in the "Tab stop position" box, and click the Set button. Publisher adds the tab to the list below the "Tab stop position" box. To remove a custom tab, click it in the list, and then click the Clear button. You can also specify how the text should be aligned at the tab and whether the tabs should have leaders. For example, if you create a table of contents for a report, you might want to set a right tab with dot leaders to draw your readers' eyes from a heading across the page to a page number. You can also set custom tabs by using the rulers. First select the paragraphs that will contain the tabs, and on the horizontal ruler, click where you want the tab to appear. Publisher places a left-aligned tab marker on the ruler. To adjust the tab's position, drag the marker to the left or right. To set a tab with different alignment, click the Tab button at the intersection of the vertical and horizontal rulers until it displays the icon for the alignment you want, and then click a location on the ruler for the custom tab. (An L is a left-aligned tab, an upside-down T is a centered tab, a backward L is a right-aligned tab, and an upside-down T with a period is a decimal-aligned tab.) When you set a custom tab, Publisher removes all the default tabs to the left of the new tab but retains the default tabs to the right.

1. Move to page 2, click the empty text box to the right of the *Adventure Works Souvenirs* story, and press **Delete**.

2. Press **F9**, and click the **Insert Table** button on the Objects toolbar.

3. Move the cross-hair pointer over the newsletter, click the upper-left corner of the empty area to the right of the remaining text box, and drag to create a box approximately as wide and tall as the text box.

   When you release the mouse button, Publisher displays the Create Table dialog box, as shown in this graphic:

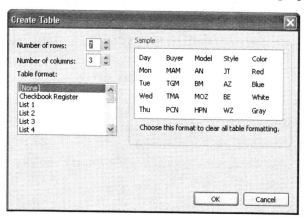

4. Type **4** in the **Number of rows** box, press **Tab**, type 2 in the **Number of columns** box, and then click **OK**.

   The table looks similar to the one shown in this graphic:

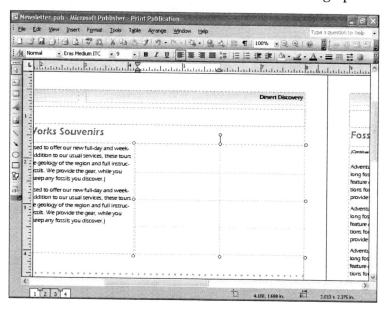

5. In the first cell, type *Baseball Caps*, press **Tab** to move to the next cell, type *$15.00*, and press **Tab** to move to the first cell of the next row.

6. Type the entries shown in the following table, pressing **Tab** to move from cell to cell:

100% Cotton T-Shirts	*$20.00*
100% Cotton Sweatshirts	*$35.00*
Tour Videos	*$45.00*

SIZING COLUMNS OR ROWS

You can change the default column widths and row heights in a table to make the information easier to read. Try this:

1. With the insertion point still in the table, point to the table's border above the second column. When the pointer turns into a downward-pointing black arrow, click once to select the column.

2. Move the pointer to the middle-right handle of the table, and when the pointer changes to a two-headed arrow, drag to the left until the column is just wide enough to display its text.

   Changing the size of the second column caused the first column to become smaller as well.

3. Move the pointer to the second column's left border, and when the pointer changes to a two-headed arrow, drag the left border to the right until it just touches the newsletter's blue guide.

4. On the **Table** menu, click **Select** and then **Table** to select the entire table.

5. Point to the boundary between any two rows, and when the pointer changes to a double-headed arrow, drag the boundary upward until the rows are just high enough for one line of text. Then click outside the table to deselect it.

   All the rows in the table change size simultaneously, and your table now looks similar to this graphic:

WORD WRAPPING IN TABLES
By default, if text in a table is longer than one line, Publisher wraps the text to the number of lines needed to display the entries in their entirety, adjusting the height of the row as necessary. If you don't want the table's cells to expand with the text, click Grow to Fit Text on the Table menu to turn off the command. You will then need to manually resize the table or its rows and columns, edit the text, change the font size, or change the cell margins when Publisher can't fit all your text in a cell.

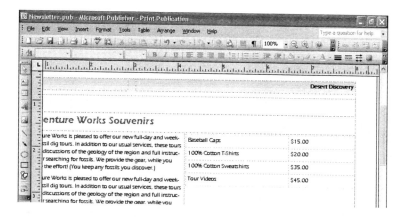

Just as with rows, you can adjust all columns of a table simultaneously without having to select the entire table, by pointing to the rightmost column in a table and resizing it.

ADDING A TABLE TITLE

Suppose you want to add a title to the table. Follow these steps to first insert a new row for the title and then format it to stand out from the rest of the table's text:

1. Click an insertion point in the first row of the table.

2. On the **Table** menu, click **Insert** and then **Rows Above**.

   Publisher inserts a blank row as the first row in the table.

3. Click an insertion point in the first cell of the new row, and type *Merchandise Price List.*

4. On the **Table** menu, click **Select** and then **Row** to select the row.

5. Click **Merge Cells** on the **Table** menu.

   Publisher combines the two cells of the row into one large cell that spans the table. The results are shown in this graphic:

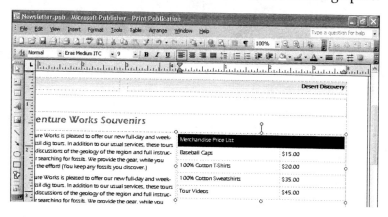

FILLING TABLE COLUMNS AND ROWS

To copy the contents of one cell to the cells below or to the right of it, select the cell you want to copy and all cells to which you want its contents copied. Then click either Fill Down or Fill Right on the Table menu. Publisher copies the contents of the cell you first selected to the remaining cells in the selection.

6. Click the **Center** button on the Formatting toolbar to center the text in the merged cell.

7. Now click the **Font Color** down arrow on the Formatting toolbar, and click the slate-blue color box (**Accent 1**, or the second box in the colors row). Then change the font to **Eras Demi ITC** and the size to **12**.

8. Click outside the table to deselect the row.

The results are shown in this graphic:

Merchandise Price List	
Baseball Caps	$15.00
100% Cotton T-Shirts	$20.00
100% Cotton Sweatshirts	$35.00
Tour Videos	$45.00

COLORING CELLS

To make your table more visually appealing, you can add color to the table's title cell. Follow these steps:

1. Click the first row of the table, and then on the **Table** menu, click **Select** and then **Row** to select the row.

2. Click the **Fill Color** down arrow on the Formatting toolbar, and click the gold color box (**Accent 2**, or the third box in the colors row).

3. Adjust the table so that it's about 2.5 inches wide and is approximately centered vertically on the text box to its left.

4. When you are finished adjusting and repositioning the table, click outside the table to deselect it.

Your table should look similar to the one shown in this graphic:

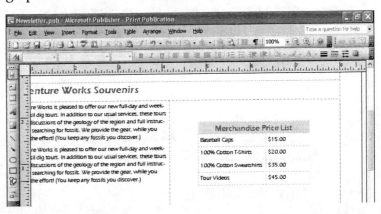

ADDING GRIDLINES AND A BORDER

To finish off the table, you want to add gridlines and a border so that it really stands out and catches the reader's eye. Follow these steps:

1. Click an insertion point anywhere in the table, and click **Select** and then **Table** on the **Table** menu to select the entire table.

2. Click the **Line/Border Style** button on the Formatting toolbar, and then click **More Lines**.

   Publisher displays the Colors and Lines tab of the Format Table dialog box.

3. In the **Presets** area, click the third box (the one that displays a sample table with inside and outside borders) to add a border and gridlines to the table.

   To add only a border, you can click the center box (the one that displays a sample table with only an outside border).

4. In the **Line** area, click the **Color** down arrow, click the slate-blue box (**Accent 1**, or the second box in the colors row), and then change the **Weight** setting by typing *2 pt*.

5. Click **OK** to close the dialog box and apply the new border settings, and then click outside the table to deselect it.

IMPORTING TABLE DATA FROM ANOTHER SOURCE

To import data from another program into a Publisher table, first open the file in the original program and copy the data. Next start Publisher. If you are copying the data into an existing blank Publisher table, click an insertion point in the table. On the Edit menu, click Paste Special, click Table Cells With Cell Formatting in the Paste Special dialog box, and click OK. If the copied text requires more cells than the table contains, Publisher displays a message asking if you want to expand the selection. You can click Yes to have Publisher expand the table to accommodate the copied text, or No to paste only as much text as will fit into the table. To insert the copied text in a new table on the active page of the publication, click Paste Special on the Edit menu, and click New Table. Then click OK to create the new table.

TABLE AUTOFORMATS

An easy way to apply formatting to a table is to use a table autoformat. Click an insertion point anywhere in the table, and click Table AutoFormat on the Table menu. In the Auto Format dialog box, you can choose from a variety of table styles. Click a table format in the "Table format" list to preview the format in the Sample box. You can modify the style by clicking the Options button and making your selections in the lower portion of the dialog box. Click OK, and you instantly have a great-looking table.

The results appear as shown in this graphic:

ADDING GRAPHS

Publisher works with the Microsoft Graph program, which you can use to create graphs and charts. To start Graph, click Object on the Insert menu, click Microsoft Graph Chart in the Object Type list of the Insert Object dialog box, and then click OK. Publisher opens the Graph program, and Graph's menu bar and toolbars replace Publisher's at the top of the window. Graph displays a grid called a datasheet that contains placeholder data, and plots the data as a graph. Replace the placeholder data with your own information, and watch as Graph updates the plotted graph. You can format the graph by changing its type, changing its colors, and adding other elements such as titles and labels. For more information about using Graph, use Graph's Help menu. To return to your publication, click anywhere outside the graph frame. You can then move, resize, and format the graph object just as you would any other object.

CREATING A TABLE OF CONTENTS

Suppose you want to add a table of contents to your newsletter so that readers can easily find the information they need. Many of Publisher's design templates include a table of contents that you can customize to meet your needs. Let's quickly fill in the placeholder table of contents on page 1 of the newsletter:

1. Move to page 1, and scroll the *Inside this issue:* table into view.

2. Replace the *Inside Story* placeholder text and the page numbers with the following text:

Adventure Works Souvenirs	2
Sandy's Stories	2
Preserving Our National Parks	2
Tour Sign-up Form	3
Fall Tours Filling Up Fast	4

3. Point to the left table border just outside the next *Inside Story* row, and when the pointer changes to a black arrow, drag downward to select the last two rows. Then on the **Table** menu, click **Delete** and then **Rows**.

4. Click an insertion point in front of the *S* in *Souvenirs*, and press **Shift+Enter** to rebreak the line. Repeat this step to move *National* to the second line in the third row and to move *Up* to the second line in the fifth row.

The results are shown in this graphic:

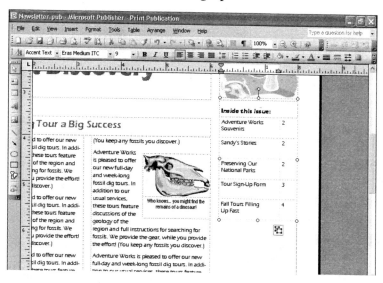

WORKING WITH FORMS

When you first created the newsletter, you told Publisher to include a sign-up form on page 3. Publisher has several types of forms that you can use as elements of publications or as their own publications. Each type of form consists of a set of text boxes and might include one or more tables.

FILLING IN FORMS

As a demonstration, let's fill in the information needed for the sign-up form:

1. Move to page 3 of the newsletter, change the zoom setting to **150%** so that you can see the text more clearly, and then scroll the sign-up form into view.

2. Replace the *Sign-Up Form Title* placeholder text with *Jeep Tour Sign-up Form*.

3. Change the heading of the middle column below the title from *Time* to *Date*. Then delete all the placeholder numbers in the **Date** column.

4. In the first **Type the event name here** box, replace the existing text with *Two-Hour Mojave Desert Highlights Tour*.

5. Select the price, and type *$45.00*.

6. Repeat steps 4 and 5, entering the information shown in this table:

Half-Day Joshua Tree National Park Tour	*$55.00*
Half-Day Old Woman Mountains Tour	*$65.00*
Half-Day Turtle Mountains Tour	*$65.00*
Full-Day Providence Mountains Tour	*$95.00*
Week-Long Death Valley National Park Tour	*$495.00*

The last tour description is too long to fit in its cell, but type the entire entry anyway; you'll fix the cell width in a moment.

CUSTOMIZING A FORM

When Publisher includes a form in a design set, it takes care of most of the formatting, sizing, and positioning details. However, you might need to customize the form to suit your publication. You can work with individual form objects or with groups of objects. In this case, you need to group the form objects and then size and move them so that they appear where you want them. Let's get started:

1. Click the **Date** text box to select it, hold down the **Shift** key, and click the **Price** text box. Then, still holding down the **Shift** key, click each of the text boxes in the **Date** and **Price** columns, including the **Subtotal**, **Tax**, and **Total** text boxes.

Publisher selects all the text boxes, surrounding them with their own borders and handles, as shown in this graphic:

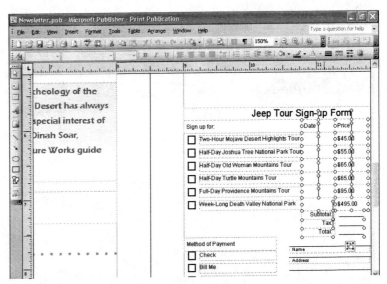

2. Click the **Group Objects** button to group the text boxes together.

    Publisher surrounds the entire group with a single border and set of handles.

3. Point to the top border, and when the pointer changes to a four-headed arrow, move the grouped objects to the right about .25 inch.

4. Click the **Sign up for:** text box, hold down the **Shift** key, click all the tour description text boxes to add them to the selection, and then click the **Group Objects** button to group these items together.

5. Widen the grouped object by dragging the middle-right handle until it touches the left side of the **Date** column.

    The description of the Death Valley National Park Tour is now completely visible, as shown in this graphic:

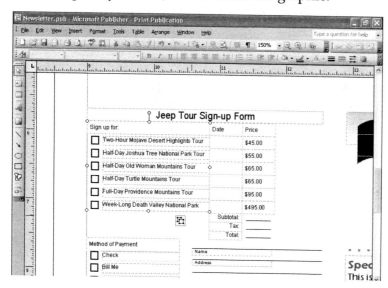

6. Scroll down the page, and click the **Adventure Works** text box below the form to select it. Then resize the text box so that it is just high enough to fit its text, by dragging the upper-middle handle downward.

    Now group the payment and address information together for one easy move.

ADDING A FORM TO AN EXISTING PUBLICATION

If you are already working on a publication and want to add a form to it, you can do so easily by using the Design Gallery. Click the Design Gallery Object button on the Objects toolbar, and then click the Reply Forms category. You can select from several styles for order forms, response forms, and sign-up forms. When you find one you like, double-click it to insert it in your publication. Then customize it by formatting it, sizing it, and repositioning it anywhere in your publication using the techniques you have learned for working with text and text boxes.

7. Click the **Select Objects** button on the Objects toolbar (even though it is already active), point above and to the left of the **Method of Payment** text box, and then drag until the pointer is below and to the right of the **Exp. date** text box.

    As you drag, Publisher draws a selection rectangle around all the text boxes between the point where you pressed the mouse button and the current position of the pointer. When you release the mouse button, Publisher selects all the text boxes inside the rectangle and surrounds them with their own borders and sets of handles, as shown in this graphic:

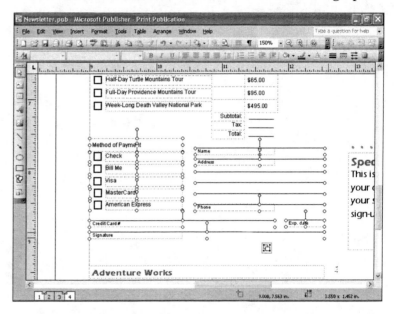

8. Click the **Group Objects** button to group the selected items together, and then move the grouped object down until it sits just above the **Adventure Works** text box.

9. Click the **Date/Price** grouped object, and click the **Ungroup Objects** button. Then ungroup the **Sign up for** grouped object.

10. Group the **Subtotal**, **Tax**, and **Total** text boxes, and move them down to make room for a new row.

    You might have to increase the zoom setting to be able to select these text boxes.

11. Click the last tour description text box, hold down the **Shift** key, and then click its date and price text boxes.

12. Click the **Copy** button to copy the selection, and then click the **Paste** button.

13. Move the new row so that it sits below the preceding row and aligns with the other text boxes. Then if necessary, adjust the position of the **Subtotal** grouped object so that it is aligned with the date and price text boxes above it.

14. In the copied tour, replace the description text with *Week-Long Mojave Desert Fossil Dig Tour* and the price text with *$610.00*.

15. Replace the text beneath the *Special Offer* heading to the right of the form with the following:

Buy two tickets for our Full-Day Providence Mountains Tour between now and June 12, 2004, and pay for only one ($95). Hurry to book your tour now. Space is limited or is already sold out for some dates.

This graphic shows the results at 100%:

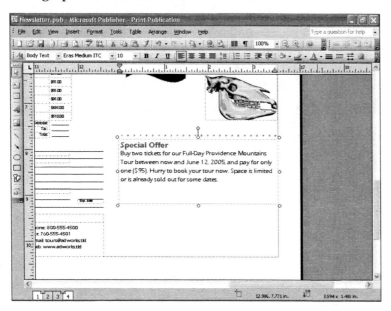

16. To see a printout of the newsletter, click the **Print** button. Then save and close the publication.

CREATING CUSTOM TEMPLATES

As you know, Publisher provides a wide variety of designs, in the form of templates, on which you can base a new publication. However, you aren't limited to these templates. You can create your own, either by modifying an existing template or by designing a new one from scratch. You might think now that you will never need or want to create your own design template. But bear in mind that many organizations use Publisher to create their marketing materials, and there is always the possibility that a competitor will select the same Publisher template and the same color scheme as you. With the skills you learn in this chapter, you will be able to create your own look and avoid potential conflict and embarrassment.

When you have finished this chapter, you will know how to:

- Create publication templates
- Add design elements
- Work with the master page layer
- Create custom color schemes
- Use custom templates

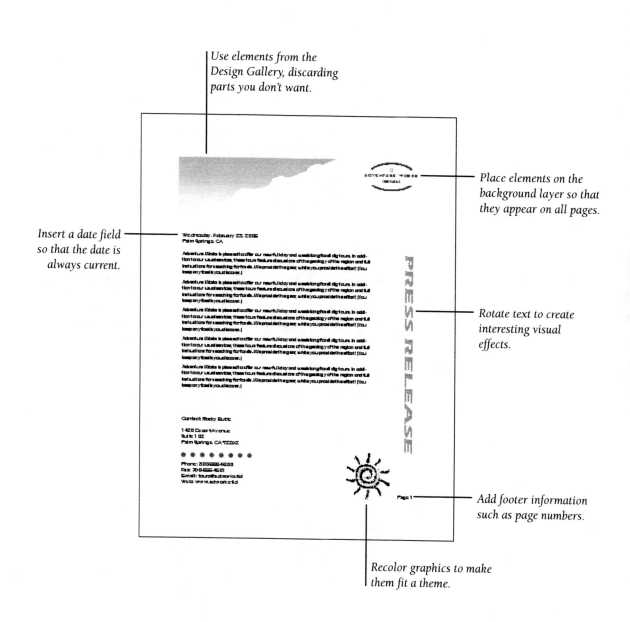

Use elements from the Design Gallery, discarding parts you don't want.

Place elements on the background layer so that they appear on all pages.

Insert a date field so that the date is always current.

Rotate text to create interesting visual effects.

Add footer information such as page numbers.

Recolor graphics to make them fit a theme.

CREATING PUBLICATION TEMPLATES

Before you start work on a new template, you need to address:

- **The design.** What elements do you want to include?

- **The look.** Should it be formal or informal?

- **The message.** What do you want to convey?

Suppose you want to create a template that can be used for the press releases that Adventure Works sends out periodically to travel agencies and local hotels. In previous chapters, you used the Waves design set and the Tropics color scheme. You still want to use elements of the Waves design to tie the press releases in with other Adventure Works promotional materials. Because Adventure Works is in the recreation business, you want an informal look, which you can achieve with the Waves design template. However, you want the press releases to attract the attention of busy travel and hospitality agents, so the color scheme needs to be livelier.

CREATING A PUBLICATION TO USE AS A TEMPLATE

You can open any existing publication and save it as a template, but in this case, you are going to base the template on a blank publication Follow these steps:

1. Start **Publisher**, and in the **New Publication** task pane, click **Blank Publications**.

    Publisher displays the layout options shown in the following graphic:

MODIFYING THE SETUP OF A BLANK PUBLICATION

You can modify the page setup of any of Publisher's blank publications by clicking Blank Publication in the New Publication task pane, clicking Page Setup on the File menu, selecting your publication type, changing the width and height, and selecting portrait or landscape orientation. When you finish, click OK to display the new publication.

OPENING AN EXISTING TEMPLATE

If you quit Publisher in the middle of designing a template, you can easily return to the template by clicking the Open button, navigating to the C:\Documents and Settings\[*User Name*]\Application Data\ Microsoft\Templates folder, and double-clicking the name of the template. If you can't see the Application Data folder, you need to make sure you're displaying all hidden files and folders. To do this in Windows XP, click Control Panel on the Start menu, click Folder Options on the Control Panel window's Tools menu, and click the View tab of the Folder Options dialog box. Then in the "Advanced settings" area, click the "Show hidden files and folders" option, and click OK.

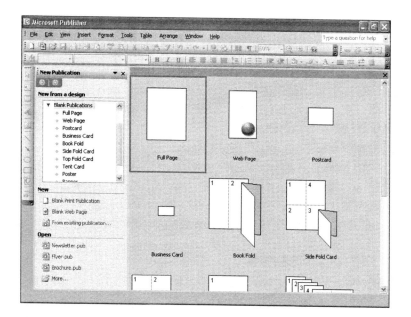

You can choose from several blank publication types, including web pages, postcards, business cards, and posters.

2. In the work area, click the **Full Page** thumbnail.

   Publisher opens a blank, 8.5-by-11-inch page in the work area.

3. Close the task pane.

SAVING A PUBLICATION AS A TEMPLATE

Before you get started with your template design, you need to save the new publication as a template. This will safeguard your changes and allow you to apply the template to publications or create new publications based on the template. Follow these steps to save the template:

1. On the **File** menu, click **Save As**.

2. In the Save As dialog box, click the **Save as type** down arrow, and click **Publisher Template** in the drop-down list.

   Publisher immediately moves to the default template storage folder on your hard drive and displays Templates in the "Save in" box.

3. In the **File name** box, type *Press Release* as the name of the custom template, and click **Save**.

STORING TEMPLATES

Publisher designates the C:\Documents and Settings \[*User Name*]\Application Data \Microsoft\Templates folder on your hard drive as the default location for templates you create. When you click the Templates category under "New from a design" on the New Publications task pane, all of the templates you have created will appear in the Preview Gallery. You can store templates in a different location, but because Publisher's default setup makes it easy to create new documents based on custom templates, we recommend that you stick with the default.

As with any Publisher file, from now on you can click the Save button to save any changes you make to the new template. (Although we won't explicitly tell you to, you should save your work often.)

ADDING DESIGN ELEMENTS

Creating a publication from a blank page might seem a bit intimidating at first, but adding the page's design elements is an easy way to get started. We show you how to look for design elements that resemble those you have in mind, add them to your template, and then customize them.

INSERTING GRAPHICS

You've already used the Waves design set in other publications, so suppose you decide to use a graphic from that design set for this template. Then you want to insert the logo you created in Chapter 3. Follow these steps:

1. Click the **Design Gallery Object** button on the Objects toolbar.

2. With the **Mastheads** category selected in the **Categories** list, scroll to the bottom of the **Mastheads** pane, and click the **Waves Masthead** thumbnail. Then click the **Insert Object** button.

   Publisher places the masthead in a frame on the blank page. You want only the wave pattern of the masthead, not the text boxes,

3. Click **Ungroup** on the **Arrange** menu, click **Yes** in the message box to ungroup the objects in the masthead, click outside the masthead to deselect all the text boxes, and change the zoom setting to **100%**.

4. Right-click the **Newsletter Title** text box, and click **Delete Object** on the shortcut menu.

5. Repeat step 4 to remove the **Newsletter Date** text box, the **Adventure Works** text box and its oval graphic, the **Volume 1** text box, and the arrow.

MASTHEADS

A masthead is the title of a publication such as a newspaper or magazine. It typically appears at the top of the first page of text. Mastheads are usually designed to be visually appealing and to catch the reader's eye. The mastheads available in Publisher's Design Gallery include the publication name, issue number, publication date, and organization name. (Publisher fills in the organization name using the information you added to the personal information set.) If you want, you can customize the masthead by adding or deleting text boxes.

6. Move the two frames comprising the yellow wave shape to the upper-left corner of the page, until the wave is top-aligned and left-aligned with the layout guides.

   You might find it helpful to use the Nudge command on the Arrange menu to position the wave shape properly. The results are shown in this graphic:

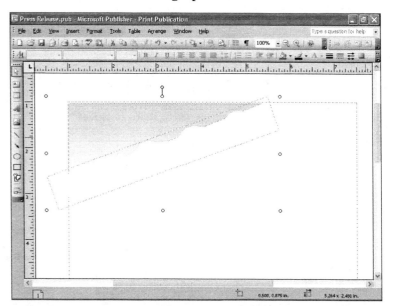

7. Open the **Brochure** publication, click the logo on the third panel of page 1 to select it, and then click the **Copy** button on the Standard toolbar.

8. On the **Window** menu, click **Press Release** to return to the template, and then click the **Paste** button on the Standard toolbar.

9. Move the logo to the upper-right corner, until its text box is top-aligned and right-aligned with the layout guides.

INSERTING A DATE FIELD

Instead of typing the date in every press release you create, you can include a date field in the press release template. This field is essentially a code that tells Publisher to insert the current date every time you create a new publication based on the template. Follow these steps to insert a date field:

1. Click the **Text Box** button on the Objects toolbar, position the cross-hair pointer in the left column below the yellow wave design element, and draw a text text box about as wide as the blue column layout guides and .5 inch high.

The results appear similar to this graphic:

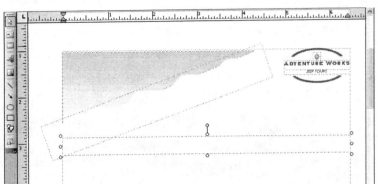

2. On the **Insert** menu, click **Date and Time**.

   Publisher displays the dialog box shown in this graphic:

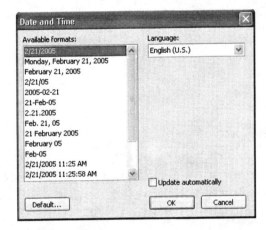

3. Click the option in the **Available formats** list that is the equivalent of *Monday, February 21, 2005*.

4. Select the **Update automatically** check box, and then click **OK** to insert the date in the text box.

   Whenever you use this template, Publisher will obtain the current date from your computer's built-in clock and display it in the press release in the selected format.

ADDING TEXT BOXES

Now that your publication has a few graphics, it's time to add some text. In the following steps, you first turn on the layout guides so that you can align new text boxes more precisely. You then create and customize two text boxes, and add a text box containing items from your personal information set. Follow these steps:

1. On the **Arrange** menu, click **Layout Guides**.

   Publisher displays the Layout Guides dialog box shown in this graphic:

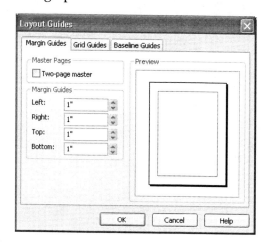

2. On the **Grid Guides** tab, change the **Columns** setting to **3**, and click **OK**.

   At 33% magnification, the page now appears as shown in this graphic:

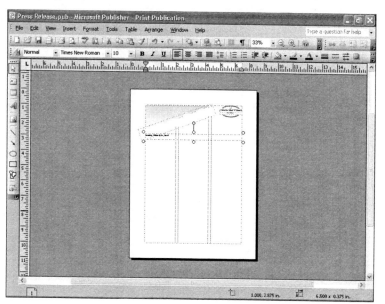

Remember, these layout guides do not appear on the printed page and, unlike text boxes, do not restrict where you can place template elements. They serve only as guides for aligning items on the page.

MORE LAYOUT GUIDE OPTIONS

In the Layout Guides dialog box, you can set the margin guides for all four sides of a page. These settings determine the position of the guides, not the position of the margins themselves.) You can also add row grid guides by entering a number in the Rows box on the Grid Guides tab of the dialog box. If your publication has facing pages and you want to adjust only the inside and outside margins of the pages, select the "Two-page master" check box. (When you select this check box, you also tell Publisher to create a left master page for left pages and a right master page for right pages.) As you make adjustments to the layout guides, Publisher displays a sample of the results in the adjacent Preview box. When you're ready, click OK to implement the changes.

3. Click the **Text Box** button on the Objects toolbar, and draw a text box anywhere on the page.

4. Type *PRESS RELEASE*, select the text, and then change the font to **Eras Bold ITC** and the size to **24**.

5. With the text still selected, click **Character Spacing** on the **Format** menu.

   Publisher displays the Character Spacing dialog box:

INFORMATION ABOUT
Character spacing, page 57

6. In the **Scaling** area, click the **Shrink or stretch selected text** up arrow until the setting is **200%**, and then click **OK**.

7. Resize the text box until all of the text is displayed on just one line.

8. To make the text run vertically down the right side of the page, click the **Free Rotate** down arrow on the Standard toolbar, and click **Rotate Right** in the drop-down list.

   Publisher rotates the text box 90 degrees to the right.

9. Zoom to **50%**, and move the text box to the right side of the page so that it sits about 2 inches below the logo and aligns with the layout guide on the right.

The results are shown in this graphic:

10. Press **F9**, click an insertion point at the end of the date field, press **Enter** to add a second line to the text box, and then type *Palm Springs, CA*. Change the font of both lines of text to **Eras Demi ITC**.

11. Move to the bottom of the page, and in the first column, at about the 7.5-inch mark on the vertical ruler, draw a text box that is the width of the blue layout guides and about .25 inch high.

12. Type *Contact: Rocky Butte*, and then change the font of the text to **Eras Demi ITC**.

13. On the **Insert** menu, click **Personal Information** and then **Address** to insert a text box containing the company's address, and change the font to **Eras Demi ITC**. Then left-align the text box with the blue layout guide, move it about .25 inch below the Contact text box, and resize the text box so that it is the same width as the Contact text box and just high enough to hold the address.

14. On the **Insert** menu, click **Personal Information** and then **Phone/Fax/E-mail** to insert a phone/fax/e-mail text box, and change the font to **Eras Demi ITC**. Position the text box about .25 inch below the address information, resize the text box so that it is the same width as the address text box and just high enough to hold the information it contains, and then click outside the text box to deselect it.

The results are similar to those shown in this graphic:

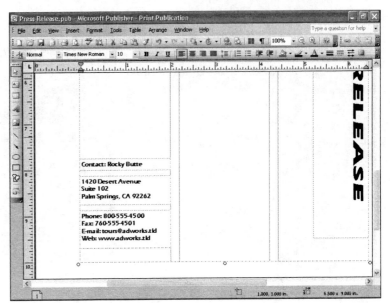

INSERTING A ROW OF DOTS

To break up the monotony of all this text, let's add a row of dots between the address and phone/fax/e-mail text boxes:

1. Click the **Design Gallery Object** button on the Objects toolbar, and click **Dots** in the **Categories** list.

2. Double-click the **Far Dots** thumbnail.

   Publisher inserts a frame containing a row of dots

3. Move and resize the frame to create the effect you want.

   You might have to increase the magnification in order to be able to see all the frame's handles. We formatted our frame to look like the one shown in this graphic:

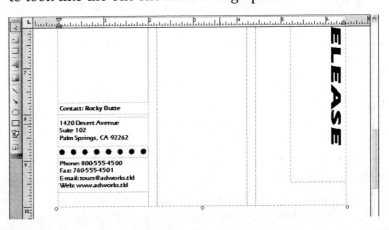

WORKING WITH THE MASTER PAGE LAYER

So far, you have added elements that will appear only on the page to which they were added. With some multi-page publications, you might want elements such as headers and footers, graphics, or a logo to appear on every page. To repeat an element on every page of a publication, you need to add it to the master page, which can be thought of as a separate layer (or background) whose elements show through each page (or foreground). In this topic, we show you how to add elements to the master page and also how to move elements from individual pages to the master page.

ADDING A GRAPHIC TO THE MASTER PAGE

You want to add a graphic to the master page of the template so that it will appear in the same place on every page. Graphics used in this way are called *watermarks*. Follow these steps to display the master page, add the graphic, and then view the effect on your publication:

1. Zoom to 50%, and scroll the window so that you can see most of the page.

2. On the **View** menu, click **Master Page**.

   So far, you've added elements only to the page's foreground, so the master page—the background—is blank.

3. On the Objects toolbar, click the **Picture Frame** button.

4. In the **Clip Art** task pane, type *weather* in the **Search for** box, click Go, and insert a graphic of the sun.

INFORMATION ABOUT
Clip art, page 93

MIRRORED AND MULTIPLE MASTER PAGES

If you are creating a publication with facing pages (such as a newsletter), you might want to have two master pages: one for each side of the spread. To create two master pages, click Layout Guides on the Arrange menu, select the "Two-page master" check box, and then click OK. Press Ctrl+M to move to the master page if you are not already viewing it. You can then add a header and footer, and they will be mirrored on the facing page. You can also add an object to one page and copy and paste or drag it to a new position on the facing page. You can create multiple master pages, rather than a two-page spread, that you can apply to different pages in your publication. On the Edit Master Pages floating toolbar, click New Master Page, assign a description or Page ID, and click OK. To apply one of these masters, switch to Publication view, and select a master from the drop-down list in the Apply Master Page task pane. To switch between master pages, click the letter or Page ID buttons at the bottom of the publication window. To view mirrored master pages at the same time, click Two-Page Spread on the View menu. You can add items to the master pages as usual in this view.

We used the sun image shown in this graphic:

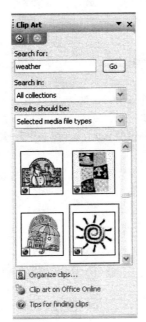

5.   Press **F9**, size and position the sun graphic in the lower-left corner of the right column, and then close the task pane and the floating Picture toolbar.

WATERMARKS

A watermark is a lightly shaded object that appears behind everything else on all of a publication's pages. To create a watermark, first add the object to the master page. Then click Picture on the Format menu, click the Picture tab, click the Recolor button, select Fill Effects from the Color drop-down list, and select a light Tint/Shade option. Click OK three times to close the dialog boxes. Finally, select any objects in the foreground that obscure the watermark, and press Ctrl+T to make them transparent.

ADDING BACKGROUND COLORS AND TEXTURES

If your publication will be printed in color, you can add color or textured patterns to the master page. To add the same background color or texture to every page of your publication, first move to the master page. To make the background color or pattern take up the entire page, draw a text box that is the same size as the margin guides. With the text box selected, click the Fill Color down arrow on the Formatting toolbar. Select a color as usual, or click Fill Effects to add tints/shades, patterns, or gradients. For graphic backgrounds, click the Picture tab in the Fill Effects dialog box, click Select Picture, navigate to the graphic you want to use, select it, click Insert, and then click OK. To make the text more visible to readers, you can either select the foreground's text and press Ctrl+T so that the graphic is visible along with the text, or you can select the master page graphic to display the floating Picture toolbar, and click Washout on the Color button's drop-down palette. To add a background color or texture to only one page, draw a text box on the foreground page, and then add the background color to it as described above. Then click Order and Send to Back on the Arrange menu to display the color or texture behind the other objects on the page.

The results are shown in this graphic:

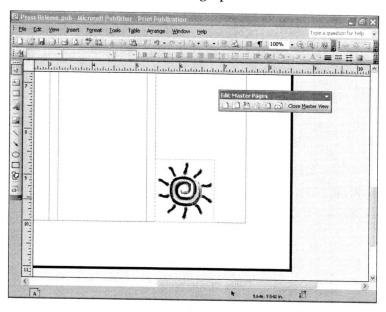

6. Press **Ctrl+M** to activate the foreground layer.

The results are shown at 100% magnification in this graphic:

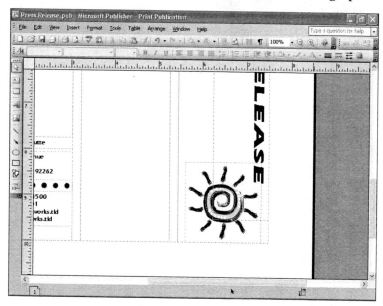

As you can see, the sun graphic you added to the master page shows through on the foreground page. If your graphic needs some adjustment, press Ctrl+M to return to the master page, size and move the graphic as necessary, and press Ctrl+M again.

ADDING HEADERS AND FOOTERS

For publications that are longer than one page, you'll usually want to add information such as the page number, date, or title of the publication at the top or bottom of every page. The information that appears at the top of the page is called the *header*, and the information that appears at the bottom is called the *footer*. You add headers or footers in Publisher by drawing a text text box on the master page and then entering and formatting text in the text box as usual. Follow these steps:

1. Switch to the master page, and if necessary, scroll the sun graphic in the lower-right corner of the page into view.

2. Draw a small text box just to the right of the sun graphic, and type *Page* and a space.

3. Click **Page Numbers** on the **Insert** menu.

    Publisher displays the Page Numbers dialog box, as shown in this graphic:

MORE ABOUT PAGE NUMBERS

If you want to add a page number to only one page in a publication, draw a text box on the foreground, and then click the Page Numbers command on the Insert menu. To omit the page number on the first page only, deselect the "Show page number on first page" check box. Also in the Page Numbers dialog box, you can position the page number in either the header or footer and change the page number's alignment so that it appears in the left, right, or center of the page.

HIDING HEADERS OR FOOTERS

If you have added a header or footer to the master page of a publication but you don't want it displayed on a particular page, you can hide it. First move to the foreground of that page. (The easiest way to verify that you are on the foreground is to drop down the View menu and verify that the Master Page command does not have a check mark by it. But Publisher also shows you which view you are in by switching background colors. In Master Page view, the background is pale yellow, whereas the color changes to gray when you are viewing the foreground.) Then if the header or footer is the only object on the master page, click Ignore Master Page on the View menu to turn off the master page for that page. If there are other objects on the master page that you do want displayed on that page, draw a text box on the foreground that is just large enough to cover the header or footer text box. When you print your publication, the empty text box will "white out" the header or footer on that page.

4. Click **OK** to apply the default settings.

   Publisher adds a pound sign (#) as a placeholder, which indicates that the program will automatically insert the correct page number on every page of the publication. (If a tippage appears with more information about this pound sign, click it to turn it off.)

5. Select the text (including the # sign), and change the font to **Eras Demi ITC**.

6. Click the **Align Right** button on the Formatting toolbar to align the text along the right margin of the text box.

7. Move and resize the text box until all its text is visible and it bottom-aligns with the sun graphic.

8. Switch to the foreground.

   The results are shown in this graphic:

9. If necessary, return to the master page to fine-tune the placement and size of the page number footer.

MOVING AN ELEMENT TO THE MASTER PAGE

What if you want to move an element that is currently in the foreground to the master page? The process couldn't be easier. Suppose you decide you want the wave design and the logo, which currently appear only a single page of the press release, to appear on every page instead. Follow these steps:

1. On the foreground, scroll the yellow wave object into view, and click it once to select it.

2. Click **Send to Master Page** on the **Arrange** menu, and then click **OK** to confirm the move.

SETTING THE ORDER OF LAYERED OBJECTS

If several objects overlap one another on the same layer of a page, you can arrange them so that certain objects appear on top of or behind other objects. Click Order and then Bring to Front or Send to Back on the Arrange menu to bring the selected object to the top of the pile or send it to the bottom of the pile of overlapping objects. Move the selected object forward or backward one layer at a time by clicking Order and then Bring Forward or Send Backward on the Arrange menu.

3. Press **Ctrl+M** to switch to the master page, verify that the wave object has indeed moved there, and then press **Ctrl+M** again to return to the foreground.

4. Repeat steps 1, 2, and 3 to move the logo to the master page.

5. Switch to the master page, and change the zoom setting to **Whole Page**. Then close the **Edit Master Page** task pane.

The results are shown in this graphic:

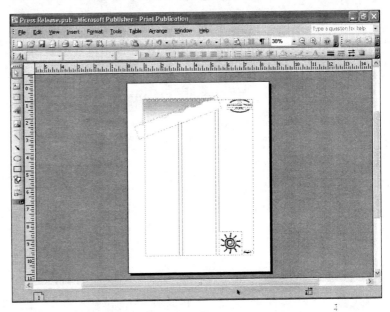

CREATING CUSTOM COLOR SCHEMES

Throughout this course, you have used one of Publisher's pre-defined color schemes to save time and ensure a professional look. However, if you always use Publisher's color schemes,

---

THE EFFECT OF COLOR

Different colors can send different messages. For example, "cool" colors such as green, blue, and violet are associated with oceans and pastoral settings and connote peace and tranquility. "Warm" colors such as red, orange, and yellow are associated with fire and heat and connote aggression and intensity. Also be aware of the following factors when selecting colors for a publication:

- Use cool or muted colors, which tend to recede, as background colors. Use warm or bright colors, which tend to advance, to call attention to specific items.

- Avoid placing red and green next to each other. People who are color-blind might not be able to distinguish between them.

- Use color to make information easier to interpret. For example, format positive numbers in blue and negative numbers in red.

- Resist the temptation to overload your publications with color. Instead, select color to focus attention on a few key areas.

your publications might start to look "canned." As you become more comfortable using Publisher, you can experiment with your own color combinations to give your publications a unique look. In this topic, we show you how to customize a color scheme.

CHANGING THE COLORS IN A COLOR SCHEME

The easiest way to come up with a custom color scheme is to select one that is close to what you want and then modify it. Let's get going:

1. Switch to the foreground, and press **F9** to zoom to **100%**.

2. On the **Format** menu, click **Color Schemes** to display the **Color Schemes** task pane.

3. Scroll through the list of colors, and click **Sunrise**.

    Publisher applies the new color scheme to the active publication, and you see the results immediately in the right pane. You want to change some of the colors in this scheme.

4. Click the **Custom color scheme** link at the bottom of the **Color Schemes** task pane.

    Publisher displays the Custom tab of the Color Schemes dialog box, as shown in this graphic:

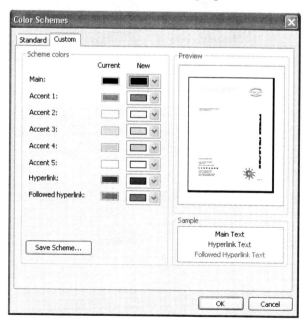

SCHEME COLORS

The Custom tab of the Color Schemes dialog box displays the main color in the active color scheme, as well as five accent colors, a hyperlink color, and a followed hyperlink color. (A followed hyperlink is a link on a web page that has been clicked, or followed.) You can use the New box adjacent to each color to change the color in the Current box. Changing any scheme color in this dialog box changes the corresponding color in your publication.

5. Click the **New** down arrow in the **Accent 1** row, and click
   More Colors.

   The Standard tab of the Colors dialog box appears, as shown
   in this graphic:

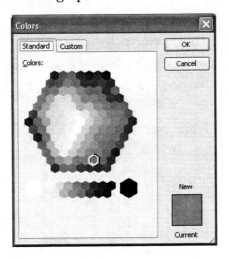

   Publisher displays a hexagonal palette of basic colors and
   indicates the current Accent 1 color with a white border.

6. Click the burgundy color (the third choice from the right
   at the very bottom of the hexagon palette), and click **OK**.

7. Click the **New** down arrow in the **Accent 2** row, click **More
   Colors**, click the light orange color (the third choice from
   the left in the next-to-bottom row of the hexagon), and click
   OK.

ADDING A CUSTOM COLOR TO THE COLOR SCHEME

If the Standard tab of the Colors dialog box doesn't provide
exactly the color you want, you can move to the Custom tab
to define the color. Follow these steps to add a custom color:

1. In the open Color Schemes dialog box, click the **New** down
   arrow in the **Accent 3** row, click **More Colors**, and then click
   the **Custom** tab.

   The Custom tab displays the options shown in this graphic:

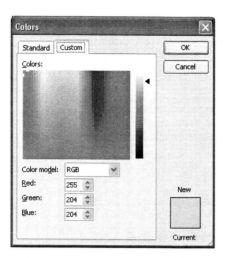

On this tab, Publisher displays a color scale so that you can select the color you want more precisely.

2. Half-hidden at the top of the color scale is a cross hair. Point to it, and drag it anywhere in the box.

 When you release the mouse button, Publisher displays the color beneath the cross hair in the top half of the New box. It also enters its red, green, and blue values—the proportions of those colors used to make the selected color—and identifies the luminance, or intensity, of the color on the vertical scale to the right of the Colors box.

3. Drag the arrow next to the vertical luminance scale up and down, noting the changes in the **New** box.

4. Take a little time to explore the Custom tab further. Then, when you're ready, use the arrows at the end of the **Red**, **Green**, and **Blue** boxes (or type the numbers in directly) to specify these settings:

 Red   *106*
 Green   *161*
 Blue   *104*

 As you enter each setting, the positions of the cross hair and the vertical luminance scale arrow change, as does the color in the New box.

5. Click **OK** to select the new color and return to the Color Schemes dialog box.

6. Click the New down arrow in the **Accent 4** row, click **More Colors**, and click the **Standard** tab.

7. Click the second brown choice in the bottom row of the hexagon, and click **OK** in the Colors dialog box and then **OK** in the Color Schemes dialog box.

   Elements in the publication that were already formatted with the Accent colors have been updated to reflect the new color scheme.

8. Close the **Color Schemes** task pane.

APPLYING COLORS FROM THE COLOR SCHEME

After you have created a new color scheme, you can apply its colors just as you would those of Publisher's built-in color schemes. Let's apply colors from the new color scheme to a few elements in the press release template:

1. Click the **PRESS RELEASE** text box, and select its text.

2. Click the **Font Color** down arrow on the Formatting toolbar, and click the green color box (**Accent 3**, or the fourth box in the colors row).

3. Scroll to the row of dots in the first column, and click the dots to select them.

4. Click the **Fill Color** down arrow on the Formatting toolbar, and click the red color box (**Accent 1**, or the second box in the colors row).

CHANGING HUE AND SATURATION

In some programs, you specify a color by changing the settings for hue, saturation, and luminance. When you specify a custom color in Publisher, you can change the hue and saturation of the color by dragging the cross hair in the color scale. To change the hue, drag the cross hair horizontally across the scale. To change the saturation, drag the cross hair vertically.

SAVING A CUSTOM COLOR SCHEME

When you create a custom color scheme, Publisher automatically saves the new scheme as (Custom) in the list of color schemes. However, the custom scheme is available only to the current publication. To save the scheme for use in other publications, open the publication containing the custom color scheme, and click Color Schemes on the Format menu to display the Color Schemes task pane. With (Custom) selected in the "Apply a color scheme" list, click the "Custom color scheme" link. Click the Save Scheme button on the Custom tab of the Color Schemes dialog box, type a name for the color scheme, click OK, and then click OK again. The custom scheme is then added to the list of color schemes available for use in any publication.

5. Change the zoom setting to **Whole Page**.

Publisher gives you a bird's-eye view of the new color scheme in place, as shown in this graphic:

INFORMATION ABOUT
Effect of color, page 158

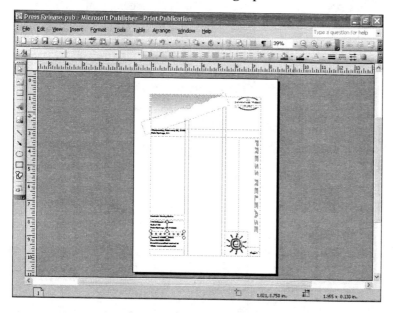

USING CUSTOM TEMPLATES

Now it's time to use your custom template to create an actual press release publication. If you have followed the instructions and saved the template in the default location, you can easily create a publication based on the template from the New Publication task pane. You can then customize the publication in the usual ways.

CREATING A TEMPLATE-BASED PUBLICATION

To put the template to the test, follow these steps:

1. Click the **Save** button to save your changes to the Press Release template, and then click **Close** on the **File** menu.

   The template closes, and the New Publication task pane is displayed.

2. Click **Templates** in the **New from a design** area of the **New Publication** task pane.

   Publisher displays the custom template you just created in the right pane.

3. Click **Press Release** to open a new publication based on the Press Release template.

In the title bar, the document name is *Publication2* instead of *Press Release*, indicating that you are working with a regular publication that is based on the Press Release template, rather than with the Press Release template itself.

4. On the **File** menu, click **Save As**, and then save the file as *Fossil Tour Press Release* in the My Documents folder.

ADDING TEXT TO A TEMPLATE-BASED PUBLICATION

Now you're ready to add some text to the press release. For this example, you add a second page, which shows you the master page elements in action. For the text, you reuse the paragraph from the newsletter you created in Chapter 4. Follow these steps:

1. Open the **Newsletter** publication, select the text of the first paragraph of the *Fossil Dig Tours* story, and press **Ctrl+C** to copy the paragraph.

2. Close the newsletter to redisplay Fossil Tour Press Release.

3. Press **F9**, and then draw a text box between the date and contact text boxes, stretching the text box across the page to the left edge of the *PRESS RELEASE* text box.

4. With the insertion point in the new text box, press **Ctrl+V** to paste the paragraph from the newsletter, and then press the **Enter** key.

5. Repeat step 4 four more times.

6. Click a blank area of the press release to deselect the text box.

The press release now looks similar to the one shown in this graphic:

MAKING TEXT BOXES AND FRAMES TRANSPARENT

When two objects occupy the same space on a page, you might want to make one of them transparent so that the other object is more visible. For example, if a text box appears in the same place as a graphic, the text might obscure the graphic. To make the text box transparent so that the graphic is visible behind it, click the text box to select it, and then press Ctrl+T. If you change your mind, press Ctrl+T again to turn off transparency.

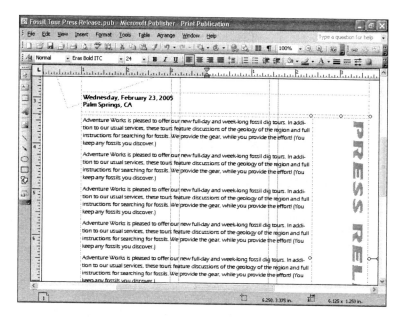

7. On the **Insert** menu, click **Page**.

    Publisher displays the Insert Page dialog box shown in this
    graphic:

8. Make sure that **Number of pages** is set to 1 and that **After
    current page** is selected, and then click **OK** to insert a new
    page after the current page.

    As you can see, the elements you added to the master page
    appear on the new second page.

9. To see the new press release on paper, click the **Print** but-
    ton. Then save and close the publication.

USING ADVANCED PRINTING AND PUBLISHING TECHNIQUES

In this course, you have created several types of publications, and along the way, we have shown you how to fine-tune their content and design. After all that hard work, you want things to run smoothly when you are ready to print or publish a publication. In earlier chapters, you clicked the Print button to print one copy of a publication, but usually your printing needs will be more complex. In this chapter, we show you more ways to fine-tune and proof your files, as well as how to handle final page adjustments for printing on paper or publishing on a Web site.

When you have finished this chapter, you will know how to:

- Make final adjustments
- Print bulk mailings
- Send publications to printing services
- Create web sites

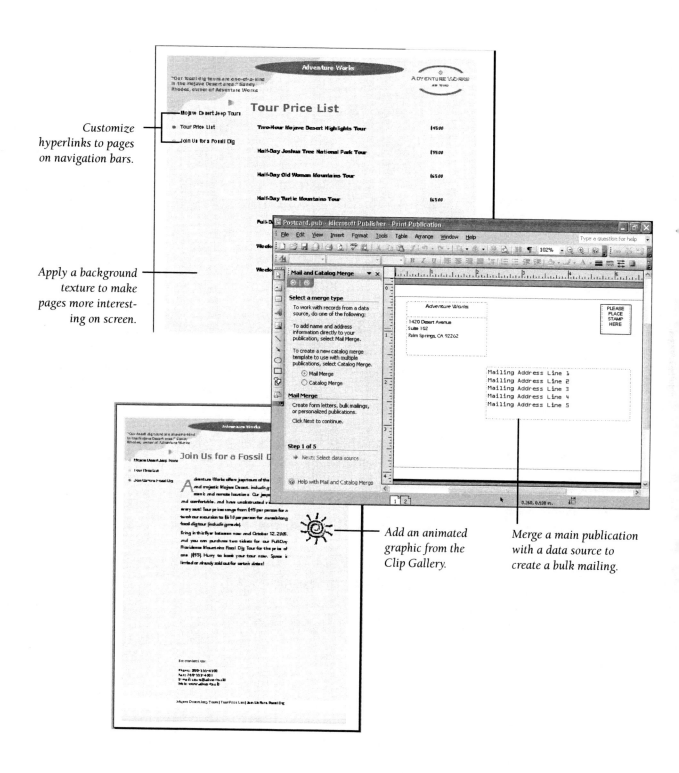

Customize hyperlinks to pages on navigation bars.

Apply a background texture to make pages more interesting on screen.

Add an animated graphic from the Clip Gallery.

Merge a main publication with a data source to create a bulk mailing.

MAKING FINAL ADJUSTMENTS

It takes time and a willingness to pay attention to detail to produce a completely error-free publication. Whether you are printing 1000, 100, or even just 10 copies of a publication, and whether you are printing with your own printer or with a commercial printing service, you can wind up wasting a lot of time, money, and resources if you don't carefully look over all the publication's pages before committing it to paper. Even if you are publishing a document to a web site, you will want to be sure that the publication will be a credit to you or your organization, and not an embarrassment. Follow these guidelines to catch most errors:

- **On-screen proof.** Look over the publication on the screen at 100% magnification to verify that it includes all the necessary information and that each component is correctly placed.

- **Paper proof.** Print a proof copy of the publication and read everything carefully, checking for spelling and grammatical errors as well as incorrect information. In spite of all the advantages of online proofing, errors are often missed on the screen but caught on paper. When you spell-checked a publication in Chapter 1, we cautioned that you cannot depend on Publisher's spell-checking and grammar-checking features to catch all your mistakes. Always read the publication word-for-word before distributing it, and if you don't trust your skills in this area, ask someone else to read it as well.

- **Proofing checklist.** For a complex publication, make a checklist of things to look for. Then check each item on the list separately. If you try to look for too many items at once, you are bound to miss something.

PROOFREADING YOUR WORK

For practice, you'll scrutinize the postcard you created in Chapter 1 as you prepare it for printing. Since you first created this publication, you have developed a logo for Adventure Works, so you want to add this missing element. Follow these steps:

1. If necessary, start **Publisher**. Then either click the **More** link in the **Open** area of the **New Publication** task pane or click the **Open** button on the Standard toolbar.

    Either action displays the Open Publication dialog box.

MAKING A CHECKLIST
When proofing a publication before the final printing, you should maintain a checklist of items to look for and then check each item on the list separately. Although proofing needs vary depending on the type of publication, certain things should always be checked. First scrutinize all the different elements in your publication for consistency of style, formatting, capitalization, and so on. Then double-check the accuracy of key elements such as names, phone numbers, addresses, and page references. Finally, check the placement and alignment of items on each page, at the same time making sure that nothing is missing.

2. If necessary, navigate to the **My Documents** folder, and then double-click **Postcard** to display it in the work area.

3. Press **F9** to change the zoom setting to **100%**, and then take a look at each element on the postcard, checking its placement on the page.

4. Read through the text, and correct any errors you find.

5. Open the **Brochure** publication, copy and paste the logo on the third panel of page 1 into the postcard, and then position the logo in the postcard's lower-right corner.

6. Select the **Adventure Works** text in the logo, and change its size to **9**. Then resize the frame until it is about 1 inch high and the same width as the phone/fax/e-mail frame above it.

7. Select the **Adventure Works** text in the oval frame at the top of the page, and change its size to **10** so that it is more visible.

The postcard now looks like the one shown in this graphic:

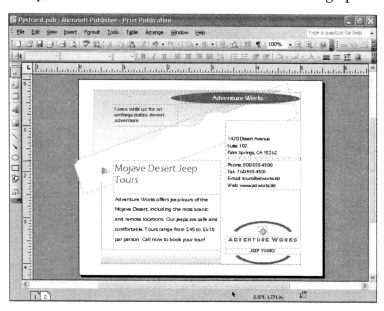

ADJUSTING THE PAGE SETUP

Ideally, you have the page setup of a publication settled before you begin working on it. However, sometimes changes you make while developing the publication can create unexpected page-setup problems, so you should always check the setup before printing or publishing. For example, suppose you are

DESIGN CHECKER

You can check a publication for potential design problems by clicking Design Checker on the Tools menu. The Design Checker task pane opens and, in the "Select an item to fix" area, displays a list of potential design problems it found in your publication. Click a problem's down arrow, and then click "Go to this item" to have Publisher locate it in the publication. If you need help understanding the problem, click the down arrow again and click Explain. Publisher displays a Help topic with more information. When you fix a problem, it disappears from the Design Checker task pane. Design Checker does not run in the background, so you should run it again before finalizing your publication. You can't rely on Design Checker to locate all design-related errors in a publication, so be sure to scrutinize it carefully yourself.

sending the postcard to a printing service and you learn that you can save money if you change the size of the publication from 5.5 by 4.25 inches to 5.85 by 4.13 inches. Let's make the change and fix any problems it causes:

1. On the **File** menu, click **Page Setup**.

    Publisher displays the Page Setup dialog box shown in this graphic:

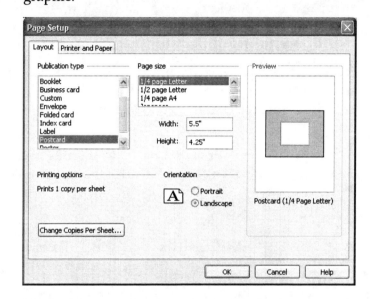

    This dialog box shows that the publication has been set up as a postcard, with preset measurements. You can change these measurements if necessary. You can also select another publication type in the "Publication type" area, and you can change the orientation from landscape to portrait in the Orientation area.

PRINTING ODD-SIZED PUBLICATIONS

If you print publications that are smaller or larger than a standard piece of paper, such as business cards or banners, you can adjust the printing options. For a smaller publication, click Print on the File menu and click the Change Copies Per Sheet button. To print one copy of the publication per page, select the "Print one copy per sheet" option. To print multiple copies, select the "Print multiple copies per sheet" option. To customize the multiple-copy setting further, adjust the numbers in the Spacing area. To restore the default settings in this dialog box, click the "Restore defaults" button. To print a large publication, click Print on the File menu and click the Change Overlap button to display the Poster and Banner Print Options dialog box. With the Print Entire Page option selected, Publisher shows how many pages it will take to print an entire publication. To change how much each tile (or page) will overlap other tiles, enter a number in the Overlap Sheets text box. To print only part of the publication, select the Print One Sheet option. By default, Publisher prints from the zero mark on the ruler, so it will print the first part of the publication. To print a different part, change the zero origin on the ruler first.

2. Change the measurement in the **Width** box to *5.85"*, and then change the **Height** setting to *4.13"*.

   Publisher changes the publication type to Custom, and updates the Preview box to reflect your changes.

3. Click **OK**, and if asked whether you want Publisher to automatically correct the wizard-created design elements, click **OK**.

   The page setup of the postcard is updated, as shown in this graphic:

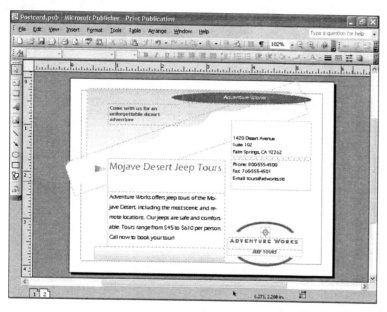

   As you look over the elements of the postcard, notice that the title and main text paragraph now wrap differently and that the web address no longer fits in its text box. Also, the logo now extends below the edge of the postcard.

4. In the title, click an insertion point to the left of the *J* in *Jeep*, and press **Shift+Enter** to rebreak the first line.

5. Size the phone/fax/e-mail text box so that the web address is visible.

6. Reposition the blue oval so that it aligns with the blue guide on the right, and move the logo so that it sits on the bottom guide and aligns with the phone/fax/e-mail text box.

7. Save the file.

The results are shown in this graphic:

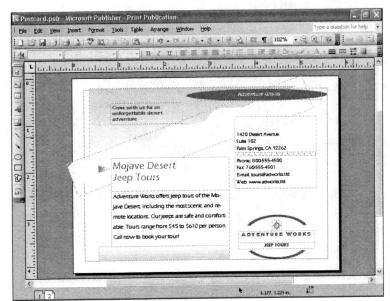

PRINTING BULK MAILINGS

If you keep a mailing list of customers, club members, or other contacts and you want to send the same postcard or brochure to all of them, you don't have to address and print each one in turn. You can use Publisher's mail merge feature to print a set of similar publications ready for bulk mailing.

The mail merge process involves two documents. You create one document called the *main publication* that contains the information that does not change from printout to printout—for example, the text and graphics of the postcard. In the main publication, you insert placeholders called *merge fields* for the information that does change—for example, the name and address of each person who should receive the postcard. (You can also insert codes that control the merging process.) You create another document called the *data source* that contains a database of the variable information.

For this example, you'll use the postcard you have already created as your main publication, but you need to create a data source. Then you can merge the two files together to print a set of publications ready for bulk mailing.

CREATING THE DATA SOURCE

If you already have a list that you want to use for bulk mailings, you don't have to create it again. You can use it with Publisher's mail merge process. If you don't already have a list, Publisher can guide you through the steps for creating one, like this:

1. With the Postcard file open, click **Mail and Catalog Merge** and then **Create Address List** on the **Tools** menu.

   You might need to install the Mail Merge feature before proceeding. Publisher displays the New Address List dialog box shown in this graphic:

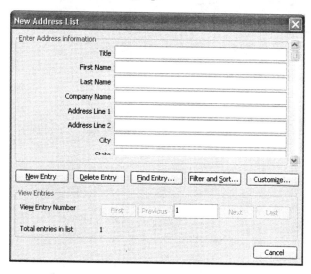

   Publisher lists all the commonly used merge field names in the "Enter Address information" area.

2. Click the **Customize** button.

   The Customize Address List dialog box appears, as shown in this graphic:

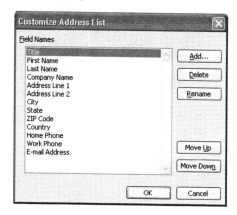

MORE WAYS TO CUSTOMIZE FIELD NAMES

In the Customize Address List dialog box, you can add a new field by clicking the Add button, typing a name for the new field, and then clicking OK. To rename a field, select it, type the new name, and click OK. To change the field order to match the order in which you enter data, use the Move Up and Move Down buttons.

3. With **Title** selected in the **Field Names** list, click the **Delete** button, and then click **Yes** to confirm the deletion.

4. Repeat step 3 to remove the **Company Name**, **Home Phone**, **Work Phone**, and **E-mail Address** fields from the list.

5. Click **OK** to return to the New Address List dialog box with the updated list of field names.

6. Enter the information shown in the following table in the indicated fields, pressing either **Tab** or **Enter** to move from field to field, and clicking the **New Entry** button to move to a new entry once you've completed the previous one:

FIELD	ENTRY 1	ENTRY 2	ENTRY 3
First Name	Erik	Michael	Dale
Last Name	Gavriluk	Matey	Washburn
Address Line 1	1504 14th Avenue SW	117 Main Street	1301 Brookline Road
Address Line 2		Apt. 5A	
City	Great Falls	Moose Jaw	San Luis Obispo
State	MT	Sask.	CA
ZIP Code	59404	S6H 1S4	93401
Country		CANADA	

When you have entered at least two names and addresses, you can use the Next or Previous buttons in the View Entry Number area to move back and forth.

7. After adding the three names and addresses, click **Close**.

Publisher displays the Save Address List dialog box, which looks very similar to the Save As dialog box.

8. Save the file as *Data Source* in the My Data Sources folder.

DATA SOURCE DECISIONS

Before creating the data source for a mail merge publication, you should think through how the data source will be used. If you plan on sorting your data, you need to put the information you want to sort in separate fields. For example, instead of a single Name field, you might want fields for First Name and Last Name. If you will use the data source for different kinds of mail merge publications, you might want to add fields that won't be used in one type of publication but will in another. For example, the first line of an address label might include a name and job title, such as Sandy Rhodes, President, but the salutation of a letter might include only a first name, such as Dear Sandy. You'll have more flexibility if you include all the information but organize it in separate fields.

MERGING AND PRINTING THE PUBLICATION

The back of the postcard includes an address text box but because the publication is not yet set up as a mail merge publication, it does not include any merge fields. Let's merge the main publication with the data source so that you can print the addressed postcards. Follow these steps:

1. Move to page 2 of the postcard, select the text in the address text box, and delete it.

2. With an insertion point in the blank address text box, click **Mail and Catalog Merge** and then **Mail and Catalog Merge Wizard** on the **Tools** menu.

   Publisher displays the Mail and Catalog Merge task pane to the left of the postcard, as shown in this graphic:

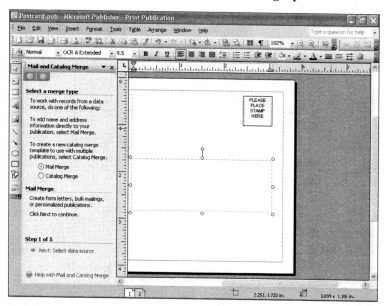

USING DATA SOURCES FROM OTHER PROGRAMS

If you have already set up a suitable table of information in another program, you might be able to use the table as the data source for mail merge publications. For example, Publisher can use information in files created with certain versions of Access, Word, Works, Excel, Paradox, and dBase. (The information doesn't have to be in a database, but it must be set up in a table or be separated by tabs or commas for Publisher to be able to use it.) Click an insertion point in the text box where you want the merge fields to appear, and click Mail and Catalog Merge and then Open Data Source on the Tools menu to display the Select Data Source dialog box. Then browse to and select the file you want to use.

EDITING DATA SOURCES

If you need to edit the data-source entries or add more entries, you can click Mail and Catalog Merge and then Edit Address List on the Tools menu, open the data source, and make the necessary changes. When you are confident that the merge process produces the set of publications you want, you can proceed to the next step.

3. With the **Mail Merge** option selected in the **Select a merge type** area, click **Next: Select data source**.

4. Click **Browse** in the **Use an existing list** area to open the Select Data Source dialog box, and select the data source file you created earlier.

   The Mail Merge Recipients dialog box appears, as shown in this graphic:

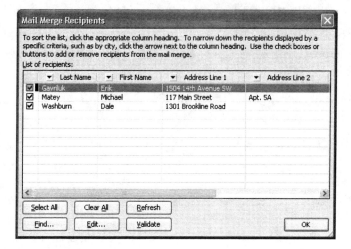

5. Click **OK** to accept the data source file with no changes, and then click **Next: Create your publication**.

USING A CONTACT LIST

To use a contact list created in Microsoft Outlook as the data source, click an insertion point where you want to add the merge fields. In Step 2 of 5 in the Mail and Catalog Merge task pane, select "Select from Outlook contacts" In the Select Contact List Folder, select the contact list you want to use, and click OK. Then click OK to accept the Mail Merge Recipients list without any changes, If you don't want to use the entire list of names, clear the check boxes of those you want to exclude. You can then proceed with the mail merge operation as usual.

FILTERING AND SORTING DATA

If your data source contains many entries and you want to merge only those entries that meet certain criteria (for example, only those with specific postal codes), you can filter the entries to extract the ones you want. Click Mail and Catalog Merge and then "Filter or Sort" on the Tools menu. On the Filter Records tab, select a field and then a comparison setting, and then type the value to compare the field to in the "Compare to" box. (You can enter up to three different filter settings.) To sort the information contained in your data source, click the Sort Records tab of the Filter and Sort dialog box. Select the field you want to sort by, and then click either the Ascending option to sort from lowest to highest value or the Descending option to sort from highest to lowest value. (You can enter up to three different sort settings.) To redisplay the entire data source, click the Remove Filter or Remove Sort button on the appropriate tab of the Filter and Sort dialog box, and then click OK.

6. Click an insertion point in the address text box, and click **First Name** in the field list in the **Create your publication area** to insert the merge field into the address text box.

   Publisher inserts a «First Name» field in the address text box.

7. Click **Last Name** in the field list.

   Publisher adds a «Last Name» field immediately following «First Name» in the address text box.

8. Click an insertion point between the **«First Name»** and **«Last Name»** fields, and press the spacebar once.

9. Click an insertion point after the **«Last Name»** field and press the **Enter** key.

10. Click the **Address Line 1** field name and then the **Address Line 2** field name, and insert a space between the two address fields. Then click an insertion point after the **«Address Line 2»** field, and press the **Enter** key to start a new line.

11. Add the **City**, **State**, and **ZIP Code** merge fields.

12. Format the new line of merge fields by clicking an insertion point after **«City»**, typing a comma and a space, clicking an insertion point after **«State»**, and typing two spaces. Then click an insertion point after **«ZIP Code»**, and press the **Enter** key to add a fourth line.

    The merge fields are added to the postcard, as shown here:

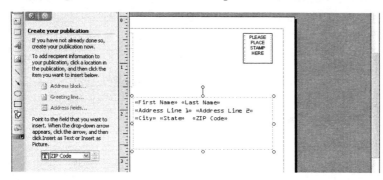

13. Add the **Country** merge field, and then click **Next: Preview your publication**.

14. Click the >> button in the task pane to display the fields for the second entry, and then click the >> button again to view the third entry.

PRINTING LABELS AND ENVELOPES

Publisher can create several types of labels and envelopes with the mail merge feature. To create a label or envelope publication, click the style you want in the Labels or Envelopes category in the "New from a design" list of the New Publication task pane. If the category does not list the label or envelope size you need, you can customize one in the Page Setup dialog box. You can then enter merge fields in the publication and format them as usual. For specific information on how to print envelopes or labels, see Publisher's Help feature.

15. When you finish previewing the data, click **Next: Complete the merge** at the bottom of the task pane.

The Mail and Catalog Merge Wizard displays the next step in the task pane. If you need to make adjustments to the placement of the merge fields before printing, you can do so directly on the page.

16. Click **Print** in the **Merge** area to display the Print Merge dialog box, which is a modified version of the Print dialog box.

17. Click **OK** to print all three merged postcards.

You can also click the Text button to print just the first entry of a merged publication so that you can check that everything looks fine on paper.

18. When the printing has finished, close the **Mail and Catalog Merge** task pane, and then save and close the postcard.

For this example, you inserted the merge fields in the order in which they appear in the list. However, you can insert them in any order or any combination. You can also manually rearrange merge fields after you have added them to a publication.

SENDING PUBLICATIONS TO PRINTING SERVICES

For a few business forms, flyers, or labels, your own printer might have enough features to get the job done. But under the following circumstances, you will need to enlist the help of a printing service, such as a copy shop or commercial printer:

- **Quality.** You need a more polished, professional look than your printer can produce. Printing services have the capacity to print in full color at a higher quality than standard office or home printers.

- **Print run.** The data source contains enough entries that using a printing service is more economical, especially when you factor in such considerations as the wear and tear on your own printer and the time it will take you to supervise the printing.

- **Special paper or size.** The publication you want to print requires special paper, such as card stock for a postcard, that your printer can't handle. Or economies of scale can be

PREPARING FOR A PRINTING SERVICE

To get a quick overview of what it takes to prepare a Publisher document for a commercial printing service, click Table of Contents in the Microsoft Office Publisher Help window, click the Printing topic, click the Commercial Printing subtopic, and then read "Prepare a publication for commercial printing." You should also check out the Color Printing topic and read about how Publisher handles color.

achieved if several copies are printed at the same time on large sheets that won't fit in your printer's paper tray.

The decisions involved in preparing a publication for outside printing are often more complex than those for printing on your own printer. However, Publisher can help you with the task of preparing your publications for a printing service. We can't cover all the details in this topic, but we do want to quickly outline the tasks that Publisher recommends you complete to maximize your chances of success.

As you read through the following tasks, bear in mind that you should complete them in order. Because the first four tasks affect the look of a publication, ideally you should tackle them before you even begin work on the publication itself. For more detailed information about these tasks, we recommend that you search the Help feature's index for topics about service bureaus and read the information given in all the topics that relate to your situation.

- **Type of printing.** Find out which types are available and which type best suits the needs of your publication.

- **Printing service.** Shop around, and make your selection based not only on price but on your feelings about the level of service you will receive.

- **Publication details.** Visit the printing service you select and discuss the details of your publication.

- **Setup.** Set up your computer and your publication according to the printing service's instructions for the type of printing you choose. For example, you might need to install the driver, or control program, for a different printer and finalize your publication with that printer selected in the Print Setup dialog box (even though that printer is not physically connected to your computer).

- **Proofreading.** Check the publication carefully, just as you would before printing it on your own printer.

INFORMATION ABOUT
Proofreading, page 168

- **File preparation.** Prepare the publication file for delivery according to the printing service's directions.

- **File delivery.** Deliver your publication in the way recommended by the printing service. For example, you might be told to deliver large files on a CD or to condense them with a program such as WinZip and then upload them to the service's web site.

USING THE PACK AND GO WIZARD

Suppose you want to send the flyer you created in Chapter 2 to an outside printing service. You've already taken care of the first five tasks in our list, and you are now ready to put the flyer file on a disk for delivery to the printing service. To make sure you don't forget anything critical, you are going to use the Pack and Go Wizard. This wizard will store everything the printing service needs on the disk, including the Unpack.exe file, which the service will use to unpack the file on its computer. Follow these steps:

1. Open **Flyer**, close the task pane if it appears, and insert a blank disk into your floppy disk or CD drive.

2. On the **File** menu, click **Pack and Go**, and then click **Take to a Commercial Printing Service**.

    Publisher displays the dialog box shown in this graphic:

3. To accept all the default settings without having to step through each of the wizard's pages, click **Finish** to start the packing process.

    The wizard goes to work, and when it's finished, a message appears to tell you that packing is complete.

4. Click **OK** to close the wizard, and then save the file.

CREATING A POSTSCRIPT FILE

Some printing services might request that you deliver your publications in PostScript format. PostScript files are used for printing on PostScript printers. Your printing service will provide you with details on how to set specific print settings, but here are the basic steps for converting your publication into a PostScript file:

1. On the **File** menu, click **Save As**.

2. Click the **Save as type** down arrow, and click **PostScript** in the drop-down list.

3. Type *PostScript Flyer* in the **File name** box, and then click **Save**.

   The Save As PostScript File dialog box appears, as shown in this graphic:

4. If the correct printer is not already displayed in the **Name** box, select it in the **Name** drop-down list.

5. If your printing service requires you to use special print settings, click the **Advanced Print Settings** button, and make your selections in the Advanced Print Settings dialog box that appears.

6. Click **Save**, and then click **OK** when the confirmation dialog box appears.

   Your publication is now saved as a PostScript file.

CREATING WEB SITES

If you need to create web pages for your organization's intranet or web site, or if you want to create pages for your own web site, you can design the pages as publications and then have Publisher convert them to the necessary HTML (Hypertext Markup Language) format. You don't need to know anything about HTML, because Publisher takes care of the coding behind the scenes.

DON'T HAVE A WEB SITE?
If you don't have access to the Internet or don't have any need to create pages for a web site, you still might want to skim through this topic to get an idea of Publisher's capabilities. Then if you want to distribute a publication that people can view on their computers without having Publisher installed, you will know how to convert the publication to HTML format so that it can be viewed in a web browser.

USING PUBLISHER'S WEB SITE CREATION TOOLS

As with other types of publications, you can use a wizard to guide you through the process of creating web pages, or you can create them from scratch. Here you create a page for Adventure Works by using Publisher's web site creation tools, which help you generate a professional-looking web page with very little effort. Let's create a simple web site:

1. On the **File** menu, click **New** to display the **New Publication** task pane.

2. Click the **Web Sites** publication category in the **Web Sites and E-mail** list, scroll through the thumbnails in the right pane, and then click **Waves Easy Web Site**.

    A new web site publication appears in the right pane, the Web Site Options task pane appears to the left, and the Web Tools floating toolbar appears. The web site currently has one page, called the *home page*, which includes text and graphic placeholders.

3. In the **Add to your Web site** area at the bottom of the **Web Site Options** task pane, click **Insert a page**.

    The Insert Web Page dialog box appears, as shown in this graphic:

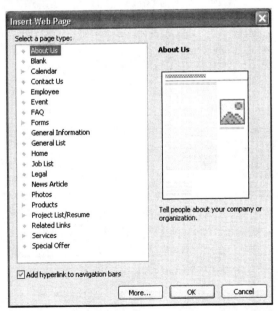

4. In the **Select a page type** list, click **Blank**, and click **OK**.

Publisher adds a second page with the Blank format to the web site.

5. Repeat the previous step, this time clicking **General Information** in the **Select a page type** list to add a general information page to the web site.

   Publisher adds the general information page after the home page and the blank page.

6. Click the **Background** button on the Web Tools floating toolbar.

   The Background task pane opens, as shown in this graphic:

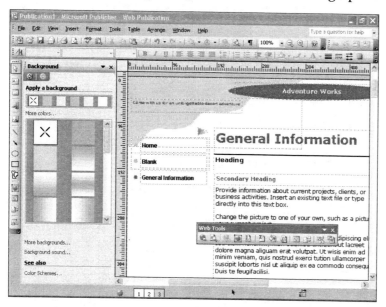

You can use this task pane to add backgrounds, colors, and sounds to the web site.

INFORMATION ABOUT
Adding sound effects, page 187

7. Click the **Texture fill (Newsprint)** gradient option (the second square in the fifth row) to add that background to the page.

8. In turn, display each of the other two pages, and apply the **Texture fill (Newsprint)** gradient option to them as well.

9. Close the **Background** task pane and the Web Tools toolbar, press the F9 key to change the zoom setting to 100%, and if the home page is not already displayed, click the **1** button in the page controls at the bottom of the work area to display the first page.

CONVERTING PUBLICATIONS INTO WEB PAGES

To turn an existing publication into a web site, open the publication, click Save as Web Page on the File menu, and in the Save as Web Page dialog box, click Save to convert the Publisher file into HTML format.

The results are shown in this graphic:

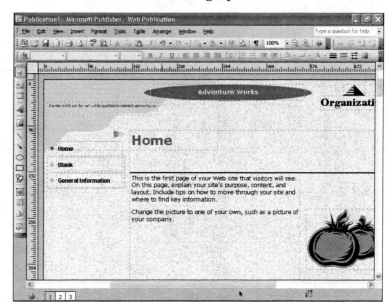

10. Save the file as *Web Site* in the **My Documents** folder, making sure that **Web Page** is selected in the **Save as type** box of the Save As dialog box.

Publisher converts the publication into HTML format.

ADDING TEXT AND GRAPHICS TO A WEB SITE

Now you can start replacing placeholder text and inserting graphics. Luckily, you use the same techniques to work with text and objects in a web page as you do when you are working with them in other publications. Follow these steps:

1. On the home page, select the **Home** placeholder heading text, and type *Mojave Desert Jeep Tours*. Then select the text again, and change its size to **16**.

2. Double-click the first graphic (the tomatoes) to display the **Clip Art** task pane, type *cactus* in the **Search for** box, and then click **Go**.

3. When the search results appear in the task pane, click a cactus graphic to insert it into the home page.

We chose the first cactus graphic in the second row.

4. Save **Web Site**, open the **Flyer** publication, and copy the first two paragraphs of the main text (but not the sold-out dates). Then close **Flyer**, select and delete the text in the text box on the home page of **Web Site**, and then paste the flyer paragraphs into the text box.

5. Close the **Clip Art** task pane.

The results are shown in this graphic at 66% magnification:

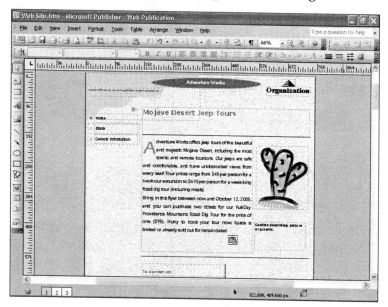

6. Before you move on, scroll to the top of the home page, and replace the logo placeholder with the logo from the **Brochure** publication.

7. Move to page 3, replace the title with *Join Us for a Fossil Dig*, and replace the placeholder story text with the paragraphs you copied from the flyer.

8. Select the text of the tag line placeholder on the left, and type *"Our fossil dig tours are one-of-a-kind in the Mojave Desert area." Sandy Rhodes, owner of Adventure Works*. Adjust the size of the text box so it is approximately one inch in height, to make the text more legible on the page.

9. Replace the logo placeholder with the one you added to page 1, and delete the **Heading** and **Secondary Heading** text box objects. Finally, add an appropriate graphic and delete the graphic caption.

OVERLAPPING OBJECTS

Whenever possible, you should avoid overlapping text boxes on web pages. Publisher treats the overlapping objects as one item by creating a rectangular area, called a *graphic region*, to contain them. Graphic regions are downloaded as one graphic and take more time to appear than separate objects. Publisher alerts you if objects are overlapping by displaying a thick red border around the graphic region. If you feel the effect is worth the longer download time, you can leave it as it is.

The results are shown in this graphic:

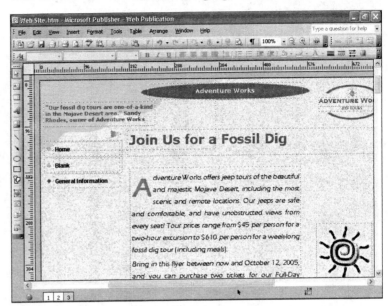

ADDING A PRICE LIST TO A WEB SITE

You want to add a price list to the second page of the web site. To speed up the process, you can reuse the information you already entered in the price list table in the brochure. Follow these steps:

1. Save the **Web Site** publication, and then open the **Brochure** publication.

2. Move to page 2, and click the price list table (not its title) once to select it.

3. Click **Select** and then **Table** on the **Table** menu, and then copy the table.

4. Close **Brochure**, move to page 2 of **Web Site**, scroll the top of the page into view, and paste the table into the page.

5. Widen the table until its left edge is approximately 1 inch from the right border of the page.

6. Change the color of the first cell's text to black so that it matches the text in the other cells of the table.

7. Delete the line breaks from all the rows, and then resize the first and second columns until all of the tour descriptions appear on one line.

INFORMATION ABOUT
Resizing columns, page 133

8. Select all of the rows and columns in the table, and press **CTRL+T** to allow the background to show through.

The table now appears as shown in this graphic:

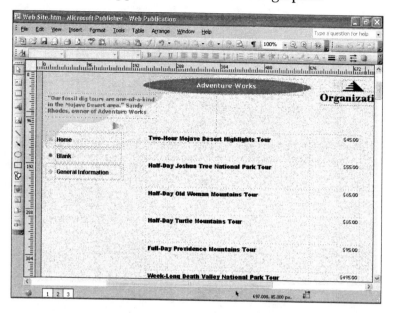

9. Copy the **General Information** heading text box object from page 3 and paste it into the top of page 2. Then replace the text with *Tour Price List*.

10. Replace the logo placeholder with the logo from page 1.

ADJUSTING INTERACTIVE WEB ELEMENTS

When you set up this web site, Publisher created navigation bars that contain three hyperlinks on each page. You can click these hyperlinks to move from one page to another. Follow these steps to make some adjustments to the hyperlinks:

1. Move to the top of page 1, and notice that the hyperlinks still read *Home, Blank,* and *General Information.*

The same pattern is followed on all three pages.

2. Select the **Home** text in the first title on the left side of the page, and type *Mojave Desert Jeep Tours*. Then replace the title for the second page with *Tour Price List* and the title for the third page with *Join Us for a Fossil Dig*.

3. Resize the text boxes until the text in each of the three hyperlinks fits on one line.

ADDING SOUND OR VIDEO

You might want to add sound or video files to a publication that will be viewed on the Internet or on a company intranet. To add a background sound to a web page, display the Clip Art task pane, check that only the Sounds check box is selected in the "Results should be" list, and then search for the sound file you want to use. To insert a video file, click Picture and then From File on the Insert menu, navigate to the file you want, and then double-click it to add it to the web page. You can then move and resize the video file's frame as usual. You will have to preview the web site in your browser to hear the sound or view the video.

This graphic shows the results at 100%:

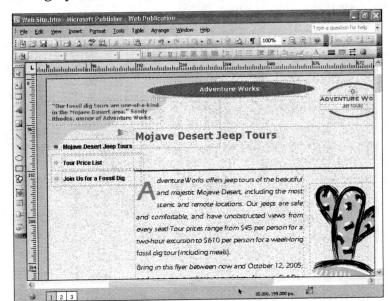

4. Move to page 2, and notice that although the hyperlink text has been updated to match page 1, the sizes of the text boxes have not. Resize them now, adjusting the table size as needed to accommodate the new size of the text boxes.

5. Repeat step 4 for page 3.

    The upper-left navigation bar has now been updated to reflect the new page titles, but the other navigation bar at the bottom of the page is still incorrect.

6. Scroll to the bottom of the page, and select the navigation bar object, then click **Navigation Bar Properties** on the **Format** menu.

ADDING HYPERLINKS

To convert existing text to a hyperlink, select the text you want to convert, and click the Insert Hyperlink button on the Standard toolbar. In the "Link to" area of the Insert Hyperlink dialog box, select the appropriate option. Then type the address of the location you want to move to when the hyperlink is clicked (or select the appropriate page option if clicking the hyperlink moves you to another page within the same web site), and click OK. Publisher underlines the text and changes it to the color designated for hyperlinks. To turn an object into a hyperlink, select the object, and then follow the procedure for text hyperlinks. To turn just part of an object into a hyperlink, click the Hot Spot button on the Objects toolbar to display the Insert Hyperlink dialog box, where you can specify the options you want.

The Navigation Bar Properties dialog box appears, as shown in this graphic:

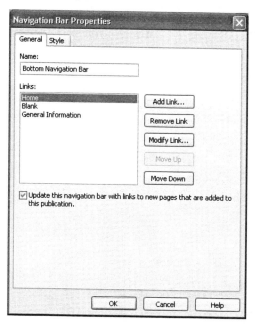

7. With **Home** highlighted in the **Links** area, click **Modify Link**.

8. In the **Text to display** box, type *Mojave Desert Jeep Tours* and click **OK**.

9. Repeat steps 7 and 8 to replace the titles for pages 2 and 3, then click **OK** to close the Navigation Bar Properties dialog box.

    The links in all navigation bars are now updated to show the correct page titles.

ADJUSTING THE BACKGROUND

As with other publications, you can easily change the color scheme, background color, or background texture of a web site. You can change the color scheme by displaying the Color Schemes task pane. However, suppose you want to change the background texture, but not the color, to something more appropriate for Adventure Works. Follow these steps:

1. Move to page 1 of **Web Site**, and click **Background** on the **Format** menu.

    Publisher displays the Background task pane shown earlier.

2. Click the **More backgrounds** link at the bottom of the task pane, and when the Fill Effects dialog box appears, click the **Texture** tab.

The dialog box displays the texture options shown in this graphic:

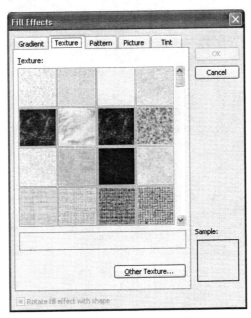

When you click a texture block in the Texture area, Publisher displays the results in the Sample box so that you can get an idea of what the change will look like. You can make other adjustments to the background on the Gradient, Pattern, Picture, and Tint tabs.

SLOW WEB PAGES

Think twice before you add too many graphic elements to web pages. Though graphic effects such as textured backgrounds can brighten up a web page, they can muddy your message, and they also take longer to download than simple backgrounds do. If you think speed is going to be important to your viewers, you might want to stick with a solid color background.

WEB FORMS

The process of setting up a web form so that it retrieves information correctly can be tricky and time consuming. Before you attempt to set up a web form in Publisher, you might want to contact your Internet service provider (ISP) for more information about their requirements. If the form you need is complex, you might be better off creating the web page in a more sophisticated web-design program, such as Microsoft FrontPage. If you want to add a simple form to a web page in Publisher, click the Form Control button on the Objects toolbar, and click one of the form control types on the drop-down menu. (For more information about the different types of form controls, see Publisher's Help feature.) You can then draw a frame for the control, enter your form's information, and move and format the control's frame as usual. (To ensure that the form works properly, do not overlap any form control frames.)

3. Experiment by clicking a few textures and viewing the effects in the **Sample** box. Finish by clicking **Stationery** (the texture that resembles sand in the fourth box in the first row), and then click **OK**.

   Notice that the Stationery texture is now selected in the Background task pane, and is titled "custom."

4. Apply the Stationery texture to each of the web site's other two pages, by displaying the page and clicking the **custom** thumbnail in the **Background** task pane.

   The results are shown in this graphic:

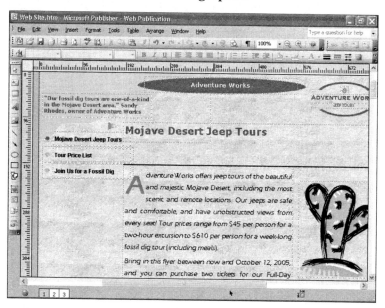

5. You decide you want a lighter background, so change it to **Parchment** on each of the pages, then close the **Background** task pane, and save your work.

PREVIEWING A WEB PAGE

When you create a publication that you will print on paper, you can see all the elements on the screen pretty much the way they will look on paper. However, when you create a web site, Publisher can't show you the dynamic elements, such as functioning hyperlinks and moving graphics. It is important that you preview your Publisher-produced web sites in a web browser before publishing them for the world, or even others in your own organization, to see. Follow the steps on the next page to preview the Adventure Works site.

SHAREPOINT TEAM SITES

Besides publishing your site on the web, you can also save it as part of a Microsoft Windows SharePoint Services team site, just like you can from any Microsoft Office program. To do so, you must be a member of the site group with permission to add items to the site. To save your file to the team site, click Save As on the File menu. In the "File name" box, enter the URL of the server followed by the name of the file, and then click Save.

1. Click the **Web Page Preview** button on the Standard toolbar.

   Publisher starts your web browser—in our case, Microsoft Internet Explorer—and displays the home page of your web site, as shown in this graphic:

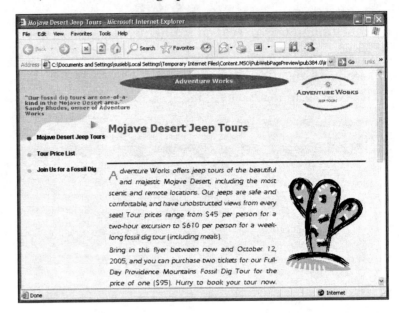

2. Scroll through the page, checking all the elements carefully.

3. Click the **Join Us for a Fossil Dig** hyperlink to check that it is linked to the correct page, and then click the **Tour Price List** hyperlink to move to that page.

INCREMENTAL PUBLISHING

After you publish a Web site, you don't have to publish every page again if you make changes to just one or two pages. Publisher is already set up by default to handle updates incrementally. If you want to change this setting, click Options on the Tools menu, and then click the Web tab. Under Saving, deselect the "Enable incremental publish to the Web" check box, and click OK.

SENDING WEB PAGES TO A WEB SERVER

When you are ready to publish your web site, you can use Publisher to guide you. With the web site file open, click web Page Options on the Tools menu. In the Keywords box, you can enter keywords (also called META tags), separated by commas, which web search engines will use to categorize your web site. (For example, Adventure Works might enter *jeep*, *tours*, *Mojave Desert*, and *fossils*.) In the Description box, enter a short description of your web site's content. When you have finished, click OK. To begin transmitting your web file to the web server, click "Publish to the Web" on the File menu. In the "Save in" box, click FTP Locations. Select the FTP site, and then click Save. (If you need to add an FTP site, you can get the necessary information from your ISP.) Publisher will then transmit the files using the File Transfer Protocol (FTP). If you prefer to use a different FTP program, click "Publish to the Web" on the File menu, designate a folder in which to save your web site, and click OK. You can then access the file and send it at any time. For more information, consult Publisher's Help feature and your ISP.